The Warrior of the West

RICHARD HUSSEY VIVIAN

David Farmer

CYHOEDDWYR
DINEFWR
PUBLISHERS

Copyright © 2005 David Farmer

Published in 2005 by
Cyhoeddwyr Dinefwr Publishers
Rawlings Road, Llandybie
Carmarthenshire, Wales, UK, SA18 3YD

The right of David Farmer to be identified as the Author of the
Work has been asserted by him in accordance with the
Copyright, Designs and Patents Act 1988.

A CIP catalogue record for this book is
available from the British Library.

ISBN 1 904323 10 3
9 781904 323105

Printed and bound in Wales by
Dinefwr Press Ltd.
Rawlings Road, Llandybie
Carmarthenshire, SA18 3YD

Contents

Author's Introduction & Acknowledgements

IT WAS INTERESTING to find that, whilst I was still in the research phase for this book, I was asked by two people on separate occasions why I was working on a biography of Richard Hussey Vivian. In each case, the implication behind the question was that I was not Cornish, and therefore that somehow I was precluded from undertaking the task. Yet, of course, more often than not, writers of biographies and their subjects tend to come from different 'camps'. One example of this is the outstanding biography of Winston Churchill which was written by Roy Jenkins; two men who came from different social backgrounds and had different political affiliations.

In the event, both of my questioners accepted the logic of the explanation, and I did not need to use an alternative or additional argument. I mention this because there may be some readers who might be asking the same question themselves. Consequently, if they felt the need for further information and I might not be available to respond, it might be helpful if I offered a second line of argument. It seems to me that this could be used on its own, or to support that which is outlined above.

John Vivian of Truro came to Swansea together with his family (without Richard Hussey Vivian, his eldest son) and, in due course, took up residence in the beautiful Singleton estate to the west of the town. Vivian's genius in running his Hafod plant was such that the family fortunes were soon assured. By that time, John o'Truro was a major figure in Swansea's nascent social circles. It would appear that the family were very aware of their responsibilities in assisting the development of the sea-port town. One of their major contributions was the construction of the town's art gallery – the Glynn Vivian. Given that name, there is little doubt that the Vivians were major contributors to the fund which established the gallery. One consequence of this was that, like many of my fellow town's folk, I grew up with the name Vivian being familiar. It was many years before I found that Glynn was not a Christian name, but a place very dear to the dynasty which emerged from there.

From my point of view, my fascination with the life of the man who was to become the first Baron of Glynn and Truro was such that I became enthralled with the task I had set myself. It seemed to me that I had the opportunity of writing the story of a true Cornish Hero; a local boy who, as his career developed, established and nurtured an ongoing, close relationship with his fellow citizens which was maintained throughout his life.

Certainly, if we are to accept the evidence from the archives, there is no doubt that he was a remarkable, greatly loved man, who achieved so much in several fields of activity but who never forgot his roots. As the writer of the obituary of this hero which was published in the *West Briton* put it:

> 'Never did we witness a fuller or more universal burst of sympathy than proceeded from the entire population of Truro on the news of the sudden and unlooked-for death of Lord Vivian. . . . His county was justly proud of him. We do not disparage the living, nor under-rate the talents and useful-ness of another generation, but where, take him all in all, shall Cornwall find his like again?'

The author of this fulsome tribute emphasised that Richard Hussey Vivian should not be forgotten! Having been absorbed by this son of Cornwall for some two years, it seemed to me that the writer of the eulogy had made a sound case for making his plea. One consequence of this was that I determined to write a book which would assist those who had forgotten Hussey Vivian to remember him, whilst helping those who knew little or nothing of him to be aware of this giant of Cornish history. His exploits in the cavalry made him a hero figure. However, the archives relating to the conscientious, dedicated service which he gave to all his appointments, e.g. Master-General of Ordnance; his sojourn in Ireland and his time as an MP indicate that there was much more to the man than his epithet would suggest.

Later in his career, Hussey Vivian made a telling contribution in support of his brother in the family firm, particularly after the death of his father. In addition, when the new company in north Wales was formed to exploit the Mona mine, he was listed as a director. As the story unfolds, the reader will perceive that Vivian's approach to life was coloured by his complete acceptance of the need to do his duty, whatever the task. To him it was a matter of honour.

ACKNOWLEDGEMENTS,
STRUCTURE OF THE BOOK AND OBJECTIVE

With the foregoing in mind, the business objective of this book is to raise funds for groups in Cornwall and south Wales which are concerned with sufferers of Parkinson's Disease and their carers. Fortunately, we were lucky enough to find a sponsor, namely MIKE JAMES, ROBERT DAVIES and the directors of the Brussels-based LIBERTY PROPERTIES who covered the bulk of the production costs involved. We are extremely grateful for that support.

'ROG', who is the artist responsible for the colour plates, painted them for a modest fee, which was much appreciated, as were the paintings themselves;

MARTIN EWENS, who designed the cover of this book and incorporated two of 'ROG's' paintings, was equally generous in setting his fee; DAVID TOVEY, another volunteer, assisted the author on several occasions with respect to computer complications. I offer my warm thanks to each of these friends.

Researching and writing the book and liaising with the publisher has been my contribution to this project. I do not accept royalties or expenses. The directors of the publishing company (DINEFWR PRESS, LLANDYBIE), printers of several books with which I have been involved over the last ten years, should also be thanked. When the organisation to whom I offered the project ignored my approach, these gentlemen took up the challenge. Their assistance is greatly appreciated. Thank you.

Numerous other people assisted me in a variety of ways. I am grateful to them all!

JEFF TOWNS (the leading Dylan Thomas specialist in the country), is another to be thanked. Jeff is, by profession, an antiquarian book dealer, and took the trouble to find me a contemporary map for inclusion in this book free of charge. The map was one of several included in *A History of the French Revolution and the Wars* by Christopher Kelly, published in London in two volumes (1819). Thank you, sir.

Numerous other people assisted the project in a various ways. and thanks are due to: MARYLIN JONES and staff (particularly GWYNNE DAVIES), of the Central Reference Library in Swansea; BERNICE CARDY and MICHAEL GIBBS of the reading room of the Royal Institution of South Wales. Michael's thoughtful gesture in alerting me to the existence of an item from the *Cambrian* which previous searching had not revealed, is typical of the interest he and others have shown. KIM COLLIS of the City of Swansea Archives reading room was also helpful at various stages in the project. Another specialist source of information came from GARY and JILL JOSLYN who advised me on the uniforms which were worn at the time of the Napoleonic wars, in order that our artist could reproduce them accurately in the colour plates. I am delighted to thank my good friend Lieutenant-Colonel JOHN LIVEING who, as ever, was my advisor on Military matters. Thank you, sir. The staff at the Royal Institution of Cornwall were also helpful on several occasions, and it gives me pleasure to thank them. They include ANGELA BROMME, ROB COOKE, and LUCINDA MIDLETON. DELYTH REES, another friend, was also helpful and I am grateful.

STRUCTURE OF THE BOOK

The initial chapter covers the period during which John Vivian of Truro set out to persuade his first-born son – Richard Hussey Vivian – to join the family firm, and, when that proved abortive, to take up a career in one of the professions. In due course, his son agreed to join a firm of solicitors in Devonport. Within weeks he had decided that the law was not for him and he joined the army as an ensign. The long march had begun.

Chapters 2 to 8 deal with Hussey's campaign experiences which reached their greatest heights at Waterloo.

Chapter 9 includes discussion on issues which two specialist Military Historians have levelled criticism at Hussey.

The final chapter considers some of the factors which influenced Hussey Vivian's life.

There follows a bibliography and an index.

Finally, I wish to salute another great man, PROF. SIR GLANMOR WILLIAMS, CBE, FBA, D.Litt, LLD, who passed away earlier this year. Prof. Williams was an outstanding historian, who, despite his eminence, was always ready to advise, suggest and encourage interest in historical research and writing. The present book had been completed in draft form just before he died, and, as with seven other projects with which I have been involved in the last decade, each chapter was read, each section considered, whilst sage advice, encouragement, and constructively critical points were made as appropriate. I was extremely fortunate to have been able to count this great man as a friend as well as a superb mentor and I am aware of many others who have similar feelings of gratitude.

Like the subject of this book, he should not be forgotten. It is in that spirit that this volume is dedicated to Professor Sir Glanmor Williams.

David Farmer

Chapter One

Finding His Way

BACKGROUND

B Y THE END of the eighteenth century, as the Industrial Revolution gathered pace, the south Wales town of Swansea attracted many entrepreneurial businessmen. Whilst these men may well have appreciated the town's beautiful coastline, the real attraction for them was its location and the impact on costs of the associated logistical factors. Swansea lay at the mouth of the Tawe,[1] a navigable river which provided sheltered anchorage for the ships that brought ores to the smelting works established there. Another key advantage was the availability of a plentiful supply of coal from pits adjacent to the town. This combination gave Swansea a head start over other locations, for it took three tons of coal to one ton of copper ore to refine the finished product. It followed that the nearer the smelting facility to the fuel the better. As a consequence, Swansea, quickly, became the copper smelting centre of the Britain. Indeed, when the 'Copperopolis'[2] was at its peak it was producing 90 per cent of the copper refined in the UK.

Among those men who moved to Swansea during that period was John Vivian of Truro (1750-1826). Together with his second son, John Henry (1785-1855), he saw the huge potential of the copper industry in the town (despite the fact that there were already five established businesses operating in the sector when he opened the new plant). Father and son were convinced that they could be more efficient than their longer-established competitors. To fulfil this ambition, in 1809 the Vivians erected a state-of-the-art plant in the Hafod[3] district of Swansea. The new plant, efficient production, and skilled management of the business and its working environment gave the late-comers such advantage that the enterprise grew faster than had been anticipated. The men who owned and ran the business must have been delighted with the outcome; they could not have wished for a better start.

Interested parties, reading the newspapers about the company's progress, would have noticed that there were several Vivians listed as its owners: the father, John Vivian, and his sons, Richard Hussey (1775-1842), the eldest; John Henry; and

Thomas (1800-21), the youngest, although Hussey,* the first born, was not involved in running the company. In fact, at the time he was serving as an army officer, which is that aspect of his life and career with which this book is primarily concerned. However, before considering his military record, it would be helpful to gain an insight into the man, Richard Hussey Vivian. The reader will thereby acquire some understanding of his character, his predilections and his development as a soldier, leader and individual. It should also reveal some of the other influences which changed him from being a young man, interested in tasting life's pleasures to the full, into the powerful personality and establishment figure he ultimately became. Without those influences Hussey might not have become a be-medalled, dashing hero, who was well regarded by the Iron Duke, was ADC to the Prince Regent, a Knight of the Realm and a Baron. In all probability a more conventional man would not have turned to his own advantage the opportunities which came his way, nor marshalled his resources in such an effective manner so as to ensure that the goals which he set himself were achieved. This is not to say that Hussey Vivian was flawless. As this account discloses, he was a human being who, like all men or women, sometimes made wrong decisions in the course of living his life.

CHOOSING A CAREER

John Vivian wanted his eldest son to join him in the family business as soon as he had finished his education. Hussey, however, had other ideas. He was adamant that business was not for him. His father tried hard to dissuade him but did not succeed. Vivian, of course, was not the only father to be faced with this problem which seems to have been endemic in the lives of many of the new breed of industrialist then making significant sums of money from their enterprises. John Vivian was as frustrated as any one of his kind, but, after exhausting all the ideas which he believed might change his son's mind, he had little option other than to accept the situation. Even so, he still cherished the hope that, at some time in the future, his son would reconsider and join the family business. Consequently, he attempted to 'keep the door ajar' by retaining Richard Hussey Vivian as a partner in the business (at least on paper). As the future was to show, John Vivian's hopes were not to be realised.

Nonetheless, despite having lost one argument, John Vivian felt it to be imperative for his son to embark upon a proper career. The father, who had achieved a great deal from a lowly start and had worked diligently in order to do so, found it

---

* Later in his career, Richard Hussey Vivian was widely known as Colonel Hussey, or General Hussey. In the following narrative the short-hand which is used when referring to him is generally 'Hussey', or sometimes 'Hussey Vivian'.

difficult to understand his son's way of thinking. It appeared to John that Hussey seemed only too eager to put the matter aside, was enjoying the life of a young buck and that it was time for him to make a decision as to what he was going to do for a living. After many weeks during which the topic of a career was raised in discussion on several occasions, the father was frustrated by the lack of progress in coming to a decision. Hussey seemed willing to put the matter aside, always making excuses about other commitments. As a result, their discussions became increasingly acrimonious. Finally, after several uncomfortable failures to reach a solution, John Vivian made it clear to his son that he was not going to keep him as an idler. It was essential, he told him, that he indicated what he wanted to do and then got on with his life.

Not surprisingly, the debate between father and son was not kept within the family; friends and business associates were aware of the tension between John and Hussey. Not that this was or is unusual, for whenever such divergences occur, it is quite common for the participants to seek comfort and support from their network of friends. It is probable, too, that Hussey's mother would have attempted to soften her husband's approach to the discussions. A quotation which stemmed from the wider literary network adds to our understanding:

> '. . . in this important matter one hardly knows whether to admire
> the liberality of the father or the instinctive sagacity of the son'.[4]

To John Vivian at the time, the idea that his son was being wise would have been difficult to accept. Like many people who are successful and achieve fame, money, and/or standing in society, it is likely that he would have equated success with his own particular approach to making progress in life. It would have been difficult for him to see merit in other routes and methods.

There was also another factor in the equation which affected the thinking of both parties: The Vivian family was Cornish but had, for the reasons cited earlier, put down roots in south Wales. Hussey, presumably emphasising his stance, pronounced himself a man of Cornwall, a position he defended until his death. At that point, *The West Briton* reported that the soldier had planned his own funeral and that his heart 'yearned for Truro'.[5]

THE ROUTE TO THE ARMY

After several months of discussions, many of which were frustrating, John Vivian was pleased to obtain his son's agreement that he should train to become a lawyer. Using his business connections, the delighted father made arrangements with Jonathan Elford, a prominent firm of solicitors in Devonport. Hussey, perhaps less than enthusiastic about the idea, started work with a view to becoming a 'counsellor learned at law'. To his father's chagrin, however, within a matter of weeks, Hussey resigned. He justified his decision by saying that he felt the law was not for him. This time, however, the son declared that he was certain he knew which career he wanted to follow. He saw himself as a soldier.

In attempting to placate his father over his abandonment of a career in law, Hussey cited his great-uncle, Colonel Hussey, who had been killed in action fighting with Wolfe on the Heights of Abraham. 'It's in the blood', he might have argued. Meanwhile, his father, once again faced with an abrupt change of mind and, probably, with less than joy in his heart, had to come to terms with what seemed to be a *fait accompli*. He must have wondered whether his son would complete anything he started? Furthermore, had he known of the circumstances which triggered Hussey's change of mind, he would have been even more concerned. The simple fact was that the reluctant lawyer, living in the garrison town of Devonport, every day saw scores of uniformed young officers, who, to him, looked as though they were thoroughly enjoying life. Among other inducements, these young men appeared to be able to attract beautiful young ladies with ease, and he decided that he would like to be part of that scene. Obviously, this information was not included among the arguments which he used to justify his decision, nor when he was attempting to get his father's patronage for help in purchasing a commission. Whatever was said, yet again, John Vivian agreed to support his son in his latest quest, a decision which may well have been influenced by an affectionate mother. Hussey was, after all, her first born.

A SOLDIER

Within days of his father agreeing to support him financially in his attempt to pursue a career in the army, Richard Hussey Vivian had obtained an ensign's commission.[6] The date for this appointment was noted in the Army List as 31 July 1793, but there seems to be some doubt as to whether he ever took up the appointment for, on 20 October, he became a lieutenant in the Independent Company of Foot. Once again that was not long-lived for, on 30 October 1793, he exchanged, once more, this time into the 54th Regiment of Foot. On hearing of these changes John Vivian must have wondered whether his son was demonstrating the same lack of determination to settle to the job in hand as he had during his schooldays. However, in retrospect his behaviour could be interpreted as showing that Hussey was beginning to develop knowledge of both formal and informal networks in the army.[7] As his career unfolded, these contacts were to prove to be an important element in enabling him to progress from the lowest officer rank to among the most senior.

Throughout the period when he was exchanging between regiments, Richard kept in touch with his parents, although cynics might argue that in a significant proportion of his letters he was asking for financial support to further his army career. There may be something in this, but his letters to the family suggest a broader agenda. For example, on one occasion he wrote from the Isle of Wight,[9] where he was awaiting orders as to his posting. Judging by the content of the letter, his father had been listening to rumours concerning the quality of the men in the army and, particularly, in the regiment in which Hussey served. The son's response left no room for doubt. He said that the officers with whom he served were first-class men, while his company of soldiers 'Go well'. In the same letter he told his father that he wanted for nothing but to be gazetted and added, as if to demonstrate that he had friends in the right places, 'the necessary forms are being signed par le Roi'. Whilst he awaited the formal announcement of his captaincy, he was taking every advantage of the island's social life. In one letter he reported that he had only dined in the mess on four occasions during one month, while there were frequent opportunities to entertain the ladies. In a letter to his father he recalled an evening when he attended a ball given by a particular general, during which one of the young ladies caught his eye. He wrote to his father:

> 'One of these young ladies was the prettiest girl I have ever seen in my life and I had the honour of dancing with her. You may depend I was not backward in calling on her next morning. Between you and me I must confess that I was desperately smitten. She, unfortunately, had no fortune, so anyone who takes her will make a bad bargain'.[10]

The philosophy of life which underlay this statement might well tempt the reader to judge Hussey Vivian harshly. But these sentiments have to be put into the context of the age to which they belong. The heartache of a girl without a dowry is a familiar theme in romantic novels of the eighteenth century. Also, given the fact that Hussey was writing to his father about a liaison with the young lady, it is possible that John Vivian was conscious that there were young maidens who might take advantage of his family's wealth by attempting to ensnare young Hussey. Such swords are double-edged.

It was in May 1794 that Hussey, responding to comments from both his parents, and presumably to assure his father that his attitudes towards progression in rank were changing, wrote:

> 'Nevertheless it is far from my mind to squander more money than is absolutely necessary. I am happy that, in four years time, I may possibly be a captain'.[11]

Either Hussey Vivian was making a subtle point about buying a captaincy, or his judgement left much to be desired, for in less than a week he obtained a company in the 28th Regiment. The new company commander, who had never seen action, found himself within days of his promotion proceeding *en route* to the Low Countries.

NOTES AND REFERENCES

1. The Welsh name for Swansea is Abertawe – the estuary of the Tawe river.
2. Stephen Hughes (ibid.), *Copperopolis* (2000).
3. Hafod is the Welsh word for a summer dwelling, or upland farm.
4. W. H. Tregelles (ibid.), *Cornish Worthies*, Volume II, Essay on Hussey.
5. Reprinted in the *Cambrian*, 24 September 1842.
6. A letter, printed in the *Cambrian*, 15 April 1881, provides us with further insight into Hussey's change of career direction. According to Hussey many years after the event, his father had 'flattered himself' that 'I might follow in the steps of my great uncle, Mr Richard Hussey (who was a very eminent Counsel) . . . He sent me to a particular friend . . . to study Law prior to my entry in the Middle Temple. But Mr Elford threw me into acquaintances with several officers of the army . . . my disposition prompting me to follow the steps of my other great uncle, Colonel Hussey . . . I was in 1793, appointed to an ensigncy in the 20th Regiment of foot . . .'

    Reading between the lines, both Elford and Hussey Vivian realised that the law was not for the young man and, using his connections, Elford opened the door for Vivian to join the army.
7. Like many other officers, Hussey Vivian purchased several of his promotions. This system enabled an officer to accelerate the achievement of their career objectives. The scheme had been developed to enable an officer who was retiring to buy a pension for himself. Since the army did not provide one, this was the only way that many officers could make provision for their old age.

    A number of commentators have argued that, whilst ill-suited appointments were made as a result of the scheme, the purchase method also allowed men to gain commands far more quickly than would have been possible otherwise. There is also the statistic that, during the Peninsular campaigns, only nineteen per cent of promotions were purchased. However, this may be a misleading figure for, presumably, far more openings for promotion were available as a result of battlefield fatalities and the 'market' would have reflected this.
8. It is interesting to note that Hussey's approach to building influential networks is hardly novel. For example, Richard Holmes in his *Wellington* explains how the Iron Duke utilised his influential connections to further his career prospects.
9. Claud Vivian (ibid.), *Richard Hussey Vivian – a memoir*. Letter from Hussey at Ironhill, undated.
10. Claud Vivian (op. cit.). Letter from Hussey at Southampton, p.7 (26/01/1794). Jane Austin's novels provide many examples of the importance of a dowry or 'expectations' to a young lady, and the unlikelihood of her being able to marry without such resources.
11. Claud Vivian (op. cit.) letter May 1794.

Chapter Two

Into Battle

HUSSEY AND HIS colleagues were part of the Duke of York's forces going to Flanders to fight against the Republicans.[1] For a young man who had been longing to go into action, the journey was something of an adventure. Unfortunately, his experience was to be far from exciting. Indeed, it proved to be a depressing début for the young captain, during which defeat was far more evident than victory. There was a severe shortage of material, food, medicine and appropriate clothing, whilst the morale of the largely inexperienced troops left much to be desired. In addition, the collaboration and co-ordination of the allies were so poor that Pichegru and Jourdan (generals in the opposing army) seemed to have the ascendancy throughout the campaign. Ypres and Charleroi, for example, were placed under siege, and continual attacks in other sectors forced the Allies to retreat. With the Republicans crossing the Scheldt, the Duke of York's demoralised troops were retreating in disorder. Hussey had gone into battle with glorious images of heroism in his mind. Sadly, the reality of the day-to-day life of a soldier in that environment was hardly the stuff of glory, glamour and honour. He found himself sleeping on the frozen ground with only a single blanket to cover him, whilst his uniform was inadequate to help withstand the freezing cold. In such circumstances it is understandable that he should turn to the warming effect of the local spirit drink. It seemed to have a therapeutic effect, and one occasion he mentioned this experience in a 'grumbling' letter to his parents. Clearly, this caused some consternation in the Vivian household, for his mother wrote back immediately with a sermon about the evils of drink. In his reply he begged her to believe that he was not growing fond of the drink. As he put it, 'I should not have mentioned it had that been the case'.[2] In that letter, he also painted a vivid picture of the kind of warfare in which he was embroiled. He wrote that he had been 'drawn into battle on fifty occasions and had been in the hot at last'.

The enemy, he claimed, were continually attacking and he had not closed his eyes for 'the last four or five days', a statement which was probably tinged with no little hyperbole. However, his assertion that 'five British Regiments, each consisting of scarcely 300 men were ill-able to defend against a victorious enemy', was not far from the truth. Perhaps reflecting his own feelings of helplessness, he confessed that he did not know what should be done. The enemy, he continued, 'in such superior force to our little army, which, damaged by frequent retreats, is very unequal to withstand them'.[3]

As conditions deteriorated, an order came from the Allied forces HQ at Dyke across the Rhine for Hussey Vivian to march as quickly as possible to cover the retreat of the 27th, 14th, 33rd, 80th and 19th regiments. In obeying that order Hussey marched his men six leagues a day for three days.[4] In his diary he noted that it was impossible to express 'The wretched state that our unfortunate army is reduced to'. Losses were significant, and in Hussey Vivian's case, at the morning parade on the day his company left Thiel, to march to Dyke, 403 private soldiers were recorded as being present. At the first parade three days later only 157 answered to their names, less than 40 per cent had survived. Soon afterwards the Duke of York left for home, with the Allied cause in tatters.[5] The army, as Hussey saw it, had suffered from poor leadership, ineffective logistical and medical support, imperfect communication and from the failure properly to feed and equip the officers and men involved. In such circumstances it would have been surprising had morale not been adversely affected.

The tone of a letter written to one of Hussey's female relatives during the campaign must have been penned when his spirits were very dejected. He became deeply nostalgic as he reached out for the familiar, the comforting, the assurance that the world he knew at home had not changed, and that he could rely on its familiar and unchanging characteristics. He wrote:

> 'If a man could perchance leave the fire and smoke and visit Truro once more, is there any chance of a fresh brood of chickens? The general opinion here is that we are soon coming home. I will visit Truro if I can, but I doubt it'.[6]

During the campaign he had tasted action for the first time. Consequently, it was only natural that he should contrast the image of battle which had inspired him with its reality in the actual warfare he had experienced. Hussey Vivian had been bitterly disappointed by the poor quality of leadership which had been reflected in many ways. Before the event, he had longed for an opportunity to take battle to the enemy, but all that he had been able to do was to help prop up a failing army. He would have to wait for some time before he experienced the tingling, thrilling, dangerous, excitement of a cavalry charge. Nonetheless, he left the Low Countries having learned a great deal, and, with a determination to be more effective as a leader of men. He swore to himself that he would try to analyse the conduct of the campaign and attempt to establish what went wrong. Unbeknown to Hussey he was in good company, for the Iron Duke, having been asked what he had learned from the campaign, is reported as having said, 'It taught me what one ought not to do, and that is always something'.[7] Thus it was that at least two men returned to England with the intention of learning from what had been something of a debacle.

Like most people who experience battle for the first time, Hussey found that his views of war had changed markedly as a result of what he had seen, heard and felt in the arena of conflict. Not that this changed his mind about continuing as a professional soldier. It was simply that, having seen men killed or maimed, particularly those with whom he had served, his conception of his profession was modified. He found, for example, that he could look at one of the great paintings of battle scenes which hung in army messes and absorb the whole of its structure. No longer was his eye taken only by the skill of the artist in depicting the glorious bravery of the central character. Now at least as important as The Colours and the victorious leader, were the dead, the wounded, the broken guns, and the discarded sabres. Hussey Vivian would not have been human had he not dwelt upon the fact that he had come through his first experience of battle unscathed. No doubt he would have thanked God for his deliverance, whilst, perhaps reflecting upon his uneasy misgivings about the extent of his own bravery in the face of the enemy. Whatever his innermost thoughts had been prior to engaging the enemy, his future career was to reveal that, if there been any, he had successfully overcome whatever uncertainties he might have harboured.

GIBRALTAR INTERLUDE

Back at the regimental home of the 28th, the usual rumours were circulating, the most persistent of which was that the 28th were bound for the West Indies, and judging by a letter written to his father, Hussey did not find the idea to be attractive. The climate was said to be unhealthy in general and made worse by indigenous fevers, which gave it a reputation as an uninviting posting. Nonetheless, it was evident that the soldier remained focused upon achieving promotion to the highest levels in the British Army. If he had to go to the Indies he would, but . . .

Once again he sought a 'diplomatic' side-step. His next move was to consider the possibility of transferring out of the 28th into a regiment which was not destined to go to the West Indies. It is clear that he had been surveying 'the market 'for possibilities, for he informed his father that he had been offered various purchases and exchanges He gave examples of the offers which he had received. It seemed that he could obtain a Majority in an infantry regiment for £1,800 or in the Carabineers for 'a regulated £3,000'. In the latter case, in return, he believed that he could get £1,800 for his company. In another letter (of 6 September 1796)[8] he sought further financial assistance. Reminding his father of the rumoured posting to the West Indies, he emphasised that, on his salary, he could not afford the necessary equipment and other supplies.

It is not clear whether or not John Vivian responded positively to that request. What was obvious from Hussey's next letter (dated 22 October 1796), was that the son had not gone to the West Indies, after all. Instead, he found himself ensconced in the fortress Rock of Gibraltar, which did not appeal to him either. In one letter he did not mince his words. Its readers were left in no doubt that Hussey was finding Gibraltar a posting he certainly did not enjoy. He felt claustrophobic there, and to make matters worse, he was not enamoured of the static rôle which the defence of Gibraltar demanded.

Thirteen years after the Great Siege (1779-1783), when the Spaniards and French had been repelled, there was, still, an ongoing threat that the Dons might attack at any time. The Governor, General O'Hara, believed it to be highly likely that an invasion would ensue very soon. Hussey had something to say about that, too. One of the issues which concerned O'Hara was the experience of the defenders during the earlier siege. At that time, enemy guns, firing from positions in the isthmus between the Rock and the Spanish forts, Philip and Barbara, had destroyed many houses in the town of Gibraltar. In several instances this destruction opened up cellars in which wines and spirits were stored, which in turn resulted in soldiers from the garrison becoming extremely inebriated.[9] In order to avoid any repetition of that, the Governor took the view that he should move the troops to the south side of the Rock, which meant that they had to live under canvas. That he made this change during the time when rain was falling (a relatively unusual happening in Gibraltar) did not help matters. There was no doubt that Hussey was unimpressed. In informing his father of the situation, he was both sarcastic and critical:

> 'A glorious campaign he made of it' (referring to the governor) . . . 'a full set of camp equipage and a wide-spread epidemical disorder amongst the troops had turned the idea of the camp into something of a crisis'. Twenty per cent of the troops involved were 'badly affected', Vivian claimed, whilst 'most of us experienced some symptoms'.[10]

By this time, Hussey Vivian's gloom must have seemed to be wrapping around him like an all-enveloping blanket. Added to that, for several months, despite having written many letters himself, he had not received a single package from anyone in England. The urgency of his need for a friendly word is best summed-up by a sentence from a letter to his mother: 'I beg and beseech you, at least once every three months to write and tell me how you are'.[11]

During this period he showed that his opinion of the Governor was deteriorating by the day. Referring to General O'Hara, Hussey said that 'he is, as usual, in a most terrible fright on account of the gun-boats . . . In fact, any man half so anxious you cannot conceive . . . and, if there's a shot fired, he will, I am convinced, be the first man killed'.[12] All in all, metaphorically if not in reality, Hussey

Vivian had come to resent (as he saw it) his misfortune in being 'locked up' in the joyless atmosphere of a kind of prison. Furthermore, according to Hussey, many of his colleagues felt as he did. He reported that they were all 'Anxious in anticipation of hearing from England, in the hopes of being ordered to Portugal' and, as he ended his letter, 'being heavily tired of this place'.

A month later, however, his spirits had been lifted somewhat, for, in writing to thank his father, his words reflected hope where previously there had appeared to be none. As he put it:

> 'I feel myself exceedingly obliged to you for the pain you have been at to procure me an exchange with the Dragoons. I am really of the opinion that, were it possible to get a troop out of the break, it would be a very desirable purchase'.[13]

Having thus shown his colours; yes, he was very interested in the potential exchange, but all the same he felt it necessary to add a *caveat*. He chose his words carefully, however for, apart from anything else, this exchange would secure his release from his 'prison'. He added:

> '. . . provided only that it could be obtained at a reasonable price but really, in these critical times, when the world seems upside down, to give a large price for any commission seems to be an imprudent thing'.[14]

It would appear that the *caveat* was satisfied, for in August 1798, presumably as a result of father's intervention, Captain Hussey Vivian had exchanged from the 28th Regiment to the 7th Light Dragoons (7th Hussars). The 'prisoner' was free.

NOTES AND REFERENCES

1. Claud Vivian (ibid.). *Richard Hussey Vivian – a memoir*. Letter from Hussey at Ironhill, May 1794, p.10.
2. In the course of the French Revolution, France became a republic. The young Corsican officer, Napoleon, fought a number of battles for the French Republican army and in 1804 was declared Emperor of France. At the time most European countries had royal families, all of whom were concerned about their future. Consequently, many alliances were formed to oppose the French Republicans and their allies. Most of the enemies of the French consisted of armies fighting to preserve the Royalist system. The British Prime Minister, William Pitt, the Younger, was an influential figure in endeavouring to keep the Royalist coalition together. Inevitably, the Republicans were seen as the common enemy by the Royalists.

3. Claud Vivian (op. cit.). Letter from Hussey at a camp near Breda dated 20 August 1794, p.14.
4. A 'league' was equal to approximately three miles.
5. This was the penultimate campaign in which the Duke of York was involved. A débacle in both this, that which followed and a seedy scandal, ensured the Duke's downfall and left him to be remembered by the satirical children's nursery rhyme, 'The grand old Duke of York . . .'.
6. Claud Vivian (op. cit,). Letter from Hussey at Bellingwalda, 26 February 1795, p.28.
7. P. J. Haythornthwaite, *The Armies of Wellington* (1994) (ibid.), p.213.
8. Claud Vivian, (op. cit.). Letter from Southampton, p.31.
9. Claud Vivian (op. cit.). Letter from Hussey sent from Gibraltar 22 October 1796, p.37.
10. See T. H. McGuffie (ibid.). *The siege of Gibraltar* (1965).
11. Claud Vivian (op. cit.). Letter from Hussey sent from Gibraltar 26 November 1796, p.40.
12. Claud Vivian (op. cit.). Letter from Hussey sent from Gibraltar 16 January 1797, p.41.
13. Claud Vivian (op. cit.). Letter from Hussey sent from Gibraltar 12 February 1797, p.43.
14. Claud Vivian (op. cit.). Letter from Hussey sent from Gibraltar 17 July 1798, p.43.

Chapter Three

To Horse and Helder

PRESUMABLY AS A result of his father's intervention, on 1 August 1799, Captain Hussey Vivian exchanged from the 28th Foot to the 7th Dragoons. As the future was to show, this was a momentous change of direction for him for, in one fell swoop, he exorcised two ghosts. He was able to leave Gibraltar; and, now that he was a horse-soldier, he was far less likely to have to serve in a static defensive situation. Within weeks he had to face up to a third ghost, for after returning to England, he found himself part of a force under the command of Sir Ralph Abercromby destined to campaign in the Netherlands. Hussey had 'cut his campaign teeth' in the Low Countries and, in contemplating the new operation as a more mature soldier, he might have wondered whether he would be more – or less – impressed by the conduct of the present campaign as compared with his experience of the other.

The Duke of York[1] was the overall commander of an allied army made up of 13,000 British officers and men and 17,000 soldiers from Russia (interestingly, all paid by the British Government). Hussey was one of only 218 horse-soldiers attached to the British contingent. By then he could claim to have been involved in the heat of battle, but was hardly battle-hardened. Given his tendency to analyse his experiences, it is quite likely that he would have thought about the negative aspects of his first campaign as well as the positive ones. Yet, judging by the letters which he wrote to his parents, he seemed not to be worried about the fact that there was a possibility that he might be killed in action, it was after the guns had been silenced that his guard occasionally dropped. The letters which he wrote after battles sometimes conveyed a feeling of tired relief. For example, in a letter dated 20 September 1799,[2] he reported that in one fierce action, a contingent of the British army had lost a quarter of its officers and men. That statistic was hardly encouraging, but what must also have concerned his parents was his statement that he was 'extremely fatigued, so much so that I cannot enter into particulars'. Their worry would have been intensified by what they read between the lines, a skill which is not uncommon within families.

Over the years, and in the many battles in which he fought, Hussey gained a reputation for bravery, which places his letters in context. Furthermore, it suggests something of his sensitivity to the concerns of others. There are those brave men who may be described as 'daredevil', who do not dwell on the outcome before acting, some are of the opinion that such people are not too bright. Conversely, when a man is creative enough to see the consequences and the implications before taking action, but is still prepared to do what needs to be done, then it is said that he is truly brave. Using this rough rule-of-thumb, since Hussey was inclined to analyse situations and visualise movement in battle, it would be reasonable to argue that he would take his place in the second category.

HELDER

The army of which Hussey Vivian was a part set sail from Deal on 26 August 1799. The soldiers left a country in which the mood of the population in general, the politicians and the military leadership was collectively optimistic about the outcome of the campaign in which both the army and the navy were involved or, to put it another way, there was the expectation that the British forces would do well. Prime Minister Pitt had, for the third time, arranged an alliance, but, on this occasion only with Russia; the Dutch refused to become involved. The mission started with a fine victory, for within three days of the allied army arriving in the Netherlands, the news came that the Dutch Navy had surrendered to the British. On land, Abercromby's first objective (to establish a bridgehead) was achieved in exemplary fashion; but, thereafter the combined army was defeated at Bergen. Within a fortnight that result was reversed, but the allied army was not able to build on its success and, following an impasse at a place called Castricum, the Duke of York took the decision to abort the campaign. It was a severe blow to the reputations of both Pitt, and the Duke of York. Within eighteen months the Prime Minister had resigned, while York was never to lead a campaign again.

Because of the earlier expectations of all concerned, the disappointment echoed and re-echoed as, not only was there was much discussion and analysis of the conduct of the Netherlands expedition in Parliament, but differences of opinion were also widespread in the public domain. Alison's reflections on the matter (written in 1860) give some indication of the strength of feeling in the country at that time. He wrote:

> 'Such was the disastrous issue of the greatest expedition which has sailed from the British Harbours during the war, and the only one commensurate to the power and character of England'.[3]

Hussey could only agree with the major criticisms being aired. He felt that the Russians were poor allies and that their soldiers were more interested in drinking and looting than fighting. If that was the case, it would have been surprising if communications between the allies had been effective. In addition, the problems which emerged as a result were exacerbated by many arguments and much ill-will particularly between the Russian and British army leadership.

All in all, Hussey felt that communication between the two allies was as poor as it had been on the last occasion he fought in the Netherlands. The same could be said about logistics (food, ammunition, and other supplies) for nothing seemed to have been done to improve matters. An example of the problems caused by these inefficiencies is recounted by Claud Vivian. It seems that a squadron of cavalry was forced to spend a night on a beach without food and water either for horses or men, an incident which must have been demoralising for the British troops.[4] Another factor which may have had a negative impact upon the morale of the British soldiers, was the absence of any support from the Dutch men. Officers and men alike may well have wondered, for whom were they fighting? Such considerations could not have been helped the officers to motivate their men or themselves.

ENGLAND, AGAIN, AND THE PHONEY PEACE

As he had done on previous occasions, in the days after the expedition had been abandoned, Hussey sought to find reasons for its lack of success. He was still pondering upon the many factors involved, when he was told that his majority was likely to be announced in the first quarter of 1800. This news helped him to salvage something from the disappointment of the expedition. Leaving aside the ineffectiveness of the Russians, as he had been obliged to do following his first Netherlands experience, he felt that poor communications and dreadful logistic management had damaged the army's ability to fight. Surely, he reasoned, something could be done to remedy these faults. Perhaps, he mused, I may have a better chance to influence matters at the planning stage at some stage in my future career.

From a personal point of view, once again he had come through unscathed, and his awareness of the brutality of battle had been heightened by that experience. This time, however, without abandoning concern for his friends, colleagues and men who had died or had been maimed in battle, he found that he was more philosophical. Even though he may have given the matter little more than a passing thought, he knew that he had come too far to abandon his profession. The likelihood of being killed in action was something with which he had to live, though, and in the not-too-distant-future (after getting married and the birth of children) he would need to reconsider the matter from the point of view of a husband and father. Meantime, he was delighted to receive his majority on March 9, 1800. In addition, even though he had been a cavalryman for a relatively short time, he had no doubt that he had made the right decision to exchange into the dragoons. He found that he greatly appreciated the ethic, the atmosphere and the camaraderie of mounted soldiery.

Few letters from Hussey were received by the family during the immediately following period, but those which were retained reveal, quite clearly, that Hussey Vivian was continuing to build his networks, whilst developing his thinking about his task as a soldier. For example, in one letter sent from Woodbridge in August 1803 he informed his parents that he had 'been acquainting myself with the coast, Yarmouth on one side and the Essex coast on the other'.[5] Like other conscientious professional soldiers, he would have wished to consider the features of a possible battleground. The east coast of England and the potential invasion threat of the massed forces of Napoleon across the channel, would have provided Hussey with the stimulus to engage in such analysis. At that stage, the scenario of an invasion of England was highly probable. Meanwhile, his letters demonstrated that he had not failed to take advantage of the opportunities which came his way to build his net-work of influential contacts. In the same letter, he mentioned some of the notable people whose hospitality he had enjoyed. For example, he reported that he had seen Sir Sidney Smith almost daily and 'I have been several times aboard *The Antelope*. He described Sir Sidney as being 'Extremely volatile and very intelligent', and added, 'Nothing, I really believe could put him into a passion'. Hussey also described an incident which occurred when he, Lord Paget, Sir Robert and Lady Harland, and a Mr Thellion were aboard *The Antelope* as guests of Sir Sidney and his lady. According to Hussey, the yacht hit a bar and, he and Lord Paget were the first to react, jumping overboard and, between them righting the yacht. The general consensus was that, had the two cavalry men not taken that action, the yacht would have floundered.

Lord Paget, who led the cavalry in the Netherlands campaign, was another whom Hussey met frequently during the 'Phoney Peace'. There were other incidents, too, which ensured that the Cornishman's reputation would be enhanced. The most dramatic of these involved Hussey, dressed in 'Full Regimentals' walking along a quay, when he saw a swimmer in the sea, obviously in distress. There were about fifty people there, most of whom were watching, but no one made a move to help. As Hussey put it: 'I jumped into the sea and had the good fortune to fetch the fellow to the shore'. The man was extremely grateful and insisted upon buying his rescuer a crown bowl of punch as a reward.[6]

With the phoney peace still holding and despite the many rumours which were circulating to the effect that the country would soon be on a war-footing again, Hussey turned his attention to romance. He met Eliza, the daughter of Phillip Champion de Cresigny of Aldborough and, in 1804, became engaged to her. Unfortunately, though, the proposed union was not blessed by either family. As a result, according to Vivian family lore, the couple eloped to Gretna Green and got married. By then, Hussey had been rewarded with a further promotion.

On 20 September 1804 he became a Lieutenant-Colonel in the 25th Light Dragoons, but, within three months he had exchanged back to 7th Hussars. At this distance it is difficult to establish the reasoning behind the pattern of these exchanges, particularly the short-lived presence in one regiment and the return to the former. All that can be said is that, in considering Hussey Vivian's career in retrospect, the tactical approach appears to have been beneficial with respect to his advancement.

In 1804, Napoleon, having appointed himself Emperor of France, realised that he would need his navy to command the English Channel if he wished to invade England.[7] Nelson's victory at Trafalgar ended that dream and, in typical fashion, the Corsican marched his 'Grand Army' from the Channel shores to the banks of the Danube. This left Britain free from the immediate threat of invasion which the location of large numbers of French troops twenty-two miles from its shores had posed. If war was to return, the newly-married Hussey must have wondered where his duty would take him? In a matter of months, he found himself destined for the Iberian Peninsula.

Having gained victories in several parts of Europe, the new French Emperor had cast his eyes on Portugal.[8] He reasoned that, using Spain as a springboard, he could invade and conquer the neighbouring country without too much difficulty. By then, the Spanish king, Charles IV and his heir had both been persuaded to renounce the country's throne and were exiled in France. In their place, Napoleon's brother, Joseph, was 'elected' as king. This decision resulted in a campaign mounted by pro-Royalist forces to attempt to oust the new regime. Meanwhile, the Portuguese royals had fled to Brazil, leaving a Council of Regency to take their place. It was this body that appealed to Britain for assistance. On 1 December 1807 General Junot occupied Lisbon for the French and, in the spring of the following year, 100,000 French troops marched into Spain.

The initial response of the British government to the Portuguese appeal was to send Sir Arthur Wellesley with an army of 10, 000 men, but it was obvious that this force was not strong enough. to match that of the French. Among those who received orders to join this second wave was Lt. Colonel Richard Hussey Vivian.

In his diary for 23 September 1808, Hussey noted that eight troops of the 7th Hussars were to be held in readiness for embarkation. It was 6 October before the convoy of ships carrying the reinforcements sailed from the Spithead, and 8 November before it arrived at Corunna harbour.[9]

NOTES AND REFERENCES

1. P. J. Haythornthwaite (ibid.). *Wellington's Military Machine*, p.111.
2. Claud Vivian (ibid.). *Richard Hussey Vivian – a memoir*, p.51.
3. Sir A. Alison, Vol IV (ibid.). *History of Europe* (1860), p.159.
4. Claud Vivian (op. cit.), p.53.
5. Claud Vivian (op. cit), p.56.
6. Claud Vivian (op. cit.), p.57.
7. J. Steven Watson (ibid.). *The reign of George III*, p.425.
8. Portugal had declined the invitation from Napoleon to join his anti-British economic sanction scheme, whereby the sale of British goods would be prohibited.
9. Claud Vivian (op. cit), p.64.

Chapter Four

Corunna, Astorga and Back

O N 7 NOVEMBER 1808 Hussey Vivian and his 7th Hussars arrived at Corunna, where they were greeted by 'deplorable' weather. As he noted in his journal, 'It rained in torrents!'[1] and, such were the conditions in the bay that many of the transports bringing the 7th to Spain were unable to tie up at the quay side. Among other things, this meant that some of the horses were obliged to swim ashore. The torrential rain and the rough sea had soaked cavalry-men and their mounts and there was little respite for both as, when they entered the town, they found that they were virtually without shelter. Many men had lost their personal kit and none of them had the comfort of a change of clothing. It was a miserable beginning to a campaign which was to prove to be unsatisfactory in many respects. Hussey must have wondered whether the weather which greeted him was some kind of omen for, in that regard, the gods had not favoured him in any of the expeditions in which he had been involved.

Fortunately, by the next day, the weather changed for the better and officers and men of 7th Hussars had the opportunity to address their problems, among which were, once again, difficulties caused by an ineffective supply system and a shortage of equipment and supplies.[2] Hussey had, he might have muttered to himself, seen it all before. Nonetheless, on the following day, with everyone working hard and with a bright sun to warm them, the world seemed to be a happier place – which was reflected the morale of officers and men. Indeed, so well did they do that, on 15 November, they declared themselves ready to march. Sir David Baird and Sir John Moore would have appreciated that news.

Immediately prior to the arrival of the 7th, the authorities received worrying news that General Blake's Spanish Army had been decimated,[3] with only Blake himself and a handful of his men escaping into the mountains. Apart from the extent of the defeat and its effect upon morale, the British army had lost a major store of supplies which had been landed at Santander. In itself that was a severe blow, which was to have repercussions throughout the remainder of the campaign.

With Sir David Baird and his army *en route* to Astorga, the command was vested in Lieutenant-General Lord Paget, the commander of the cavalry. It was on 15 November that the First Division of the 7th Hussars began its march to Astorga. Hussey followed at the head of the Third Division two days later. It was

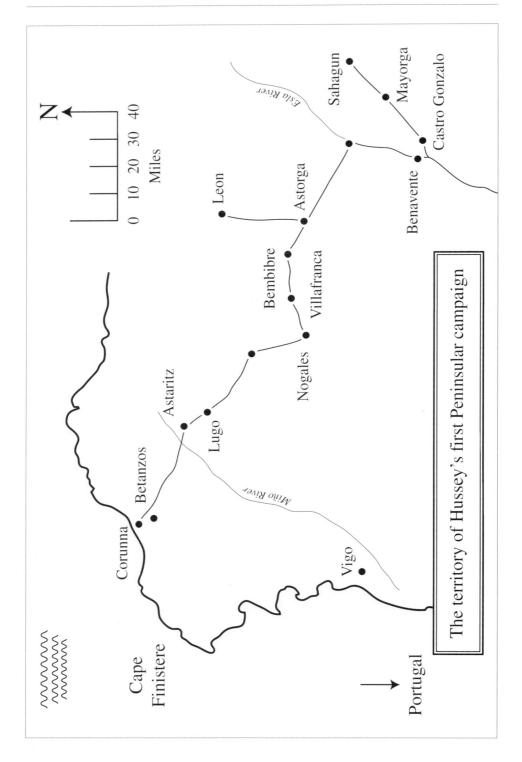

The territory of Hussey's first Peninsular campaign

fortunate that they marched in fine weather and, despite losing horses during the journey, the warmer air was beneficial to man and beast in terms of both physical well-being and morale.

When he first disembarked at Corunna, Lieutenant-General Lord Paget, who commanded the cavalry, received 'an express' from Sir David Baird requesting him to proceed, without delay, to a place called Astorga. The intention was to support Baird and assist in forging a link between his army and that of Sir John Moore. The cavalry officers were briefed about the terrain, why Astorga was to be the rallying point, and where they would aim to unite the two armies. A transit plan was developed, which allowed a total of thirteen days (two of which were rest days) to cover the distance. Given the urgency of the call for reinforcements, this was no longer valid; the cavalry would need, not only to forego the rest days, but to travel more quickly than they had planned. It was vital that they should arrive at Astorga as soon as possible, for it was the general consensus of opinion that the French, with a significantly larger force, would march on that town as soon as they had completed their preparations. As Sir David Baird put it in his 'express', 'I find myself in a most critical situation'.[4]

Unfortunately, the horses of the Hussars began to drop out even before the march began and continued to do so during its various stages. Twelve were lost before leaving Corunna and a further seventy-five became lame. Hussey believed that the animals had been made to work hard too soon after their thirty-five day confinement aboard ship in transit from Spithead, but in the circumstances, there was little that anyone could do to solve the problem. Furthermore, the poor quality of forage which was available to them was hardly conducive to their good health. Overall, the poor condition of the horses meant, that there would be fewer cavalry men to assist the British cause, though, no doubt, Baird would settle for that, provided that those which remained fit for duty arrived on time.

Fortunately, *en route*, Hussey Vivian was well-mounted and he and his fellow officers and troops, made good time, and that despite the fact that he had felt ill before leaving Corunna. In his diary, Hussey noted that he was feeling extremely feverish and unwell but, since the 7th Hussars had been given the accolade of being in advance of the main body of cavalry he 'could not think of failing Lord Paget'.[5]

When Paget's men reached their first objective, they were greeted with the news that Blake's Spanish army was in disarray and that, when they arrived at Astorga they would only find remnants of a once-proud body of men. They were further dismayed by intelligence, received at the time of their arrival, which forecast that the French were massing in readiness to drive a wedge between the armies of Baird and Moore. It was said that on 5 November, Napoleon had arrived in person, and that he had every intention of bringing the Spanish War to an end by means of a major victory. His army of 150,000 men, when assembled, was seen to be such a threat that Sir John Moore opted to withdraw. However, on November 28, Portuguese and Spanish diplomats pleaded with their British counterpart not to abandon them when Napoleon was on their doorstep.

A week later, Moore who had listened to the heartfelt pleas of the representatives of both Spain and Portugal,[6] and having been assured that they would fight on, decided to advance towards the French. In particular, he wanted to relieve the pressure on Madrid which, he had been told, was going to make a stand against the Napoleon. Unfortunately, the Spanish garrison at Madrid capitulated without a shot being fired and, that despite the fact that they had pleaded for support on the day before their surrender. What was equally galling was that nobody had given a thought to informing Moore. As a consequence, the general assumed that the Spaniards would make a stand, and as a result, continued to advance towards the French.

The widely-held opinion among the British officers at this time was that, once he had assembled his army, Napoleon would utilise its power to try to crush the British and drive them out from the Iberian Peninsula. Having considered the many factors in the situation carefully, Sir John Moore and Sir David Baird ordered a controlled withdrawal, with the troops being ready to evacuate through the port of Corunna. Lord Paget, Hussey Vivian and their colleagues were assigned to contribute to the rearguard action which was a vital factor in allowing the main body of the British forces to retreat in good order.

RETREAT

Subsequently, as Hussey noted in his journal,[7] it was admitted by 'higher authorities' that had he (Moore) stayed just one day longer, his army would have been cut off by the French. Sir John Moore's retreat commenced on 24 December 1808, three days before Lord Paget attacked a French regiment at Sahagun. The cavalry commander had planned to strike in the early hours of the morning (in order to gain the benefit of surprise), and did so despite the fact that the enemy had been forewarned. In a brilliantly executed attack, Paget's force routed the French, killing or wounding some 200 of their officers and men.[8] There is little doubt that his triumph considerably diminished the propensity of the French units to attack the retreating British army. Paget's audacity and verve in gaining this victory having instilled serious doubts in the enemy's minds.

Meantime, Hussey had received orders to go to a particular location to rendezvous with another party. Having arrived there, however, he found no one else in the vicinity.[9] He sent a message back to Lord Paget, who instructed him to quarter his troops in a near-by village *pro tem*. When Hussey and his troops arrived there, he learned that a French force of 600 men was camped in one of the other adjacent hamlets. According to his informant, the French had cavalry, infantry and artillery. At that time, the 7th regiment had just 380 mounted men, so it was clear that Hussey was outnumbered and had inferior resources. Nevertheless, he believed that he could strike a blow which would help to slow the advance of the French by inducing them to believe that the strength of the British force was greater than it actually was. Following the basic principles of warfare, before committing his force to action, he sent a patrol to confirm the enemy's strength. Whilst the patrol was about its business, Brigadier-General Stewart arrived and, to Hussey's disappointment, stated that he did not consider himself to be authorised to make the decision to attack.

The following day, Lieut-Colonel Otway, with only 130 men, charged the French and stopped them in their tracks. Unfortunately, the impetuosity of the Hussars caused them to follow through, after which, in order, to avoid being cut-off, they were forced to withdraw. This was a pity, yet in having to deal with that thrust, the French had learned something about the ability of the British cavalry and doubts might well have been planted in their minds. On re-forming, Otway's troops were joined by Stewart, who had a hundred Germans under his command, and the combined force charged again. If the French were cautious after Otway's attack, they would have been doubly so when Stewart and his men combined with him to strike at the French again. Having been informed of the action, Lord Paget was next to arrive and, in order to allow him to bring up the 10th Hussars, ordered Otway and Stewart to keep the French in check. Soon after he called up the 7th, who returned with the 18th and two pieces of light artillery.

If they had doubted the British strength before, these reinforcements must have increased the consternation in the minds of the French. Seeing the additional men and guns, they turned tail and hurried back to the river where, in struggling to escape across the water, many of them were caught by Paget's Hussars. Hundreds of the elite French corps. were killed and Paget's Hussars took a hundred prisoners, among whom was Lieut-General Lefevre-Desnouettes,[10] one of Napoleon's most senior cavalry officers. Lefevre surrendered to two private soldiers, one from the 7th Hussars and the other from the 10th.

After the dust had settled, the 7th were instructed to remain (with the two pieces of artillery),[11] whilst the rest returned to Benavente. The French, meantime, had withdrawn, having seen their *Chasseurs a cheval de la Garde Imperiale* beaten conclusively. They would be far more cautious about attacking the British again, and there followed a period during which little of consequence took place. Occasionally the head of a column of cavalry would emerge as if testing the alertness of the British troops. Whenever that occurred, an artillery shot seemed to be sufficient to have them scuttling back. At that point in the affair, the 7th were admirably achieving the objective of an effective rearguard; slow down the enemy and give as much time as possible for the retreating army to make its way to safety. It was during the period when the 7th, officers and men were on duty near the river, that Hussey made a decision which, afterwards he regretted. At about mid-day, following a quiet morning, Hussey and his colleagues saw a figure on the hill immediately above them. Through the glass, the man, who had an entourage of some size, who wore the uniform of a general and who had a stocky figure, was obviously surveying the British position. Given the assumption that it was none other than Napoleon, the officer commanding the artillery asked Hussey for permission to take a shot at the man.[12] Hussey, however, refused, but when the French party moved off, he regretted his decision. As he wrote in his journal:

> 'Despising a war of outposts, I declined it. I afterwards rather regretted having done so, when I reflected, if it had been Bonaparte and should a shot have been successful, on the benefit that would have resulted to the world in general and I, in consequence accused myself of having, from motives of humanity, avoided doing that which would have contributed so much happiness to mankind'.[13]

In due course, the 18th Hussars relieved Hussey's men, who briefed the incomers in the usual way, warning them that the French had called up some artillery but that, despite the potential of their guns, up to that point, the enemy had been ineffective. Having held up the French for a valuable period, the 18th and the 7th marched to La Benaza and then on to Astorga. The French, having broken through in several places quickly took control of Leon (just 25 miles from Astorga), so on the evening of the last day of December 1808, with the French snapping at their heels, the two regiments withdrew from Astorga and marched without halting to Bembibre, which was 24 miles away in a westerly direction. Hussey called the march 'very tedious and severe'.[14] In one section, for example, men and horses had to walk over a sizeable mountain upon which considerable snow had fallen and over which the infantry had marched. This resulted in some very slippery sections where the Hussars were obliged to lead their horses.

On New Year's Day the 7th were with the main body of the army, whilst the 15th were undertaking the rearguard task. By this time the French had regained some confidence and the British were having to deal with repeated skirmishing. Whilst the news that Napoleon had left for Paris was received with some enthusiasm, the fact that his army of 60,000 had entered Astorga, with two very experienced generals in charge (Soult and Ney), was little comfort to the retreating British army which, by then, was only 20,000 strong.

The next march of Hussey's 7th took the regiment from Villafranca to Lugo. Once again, the route taken included a huge mountain but, this time not only were the conditions underfoot difficult, it was also freezing cold, a combination which, together with fatigue, resulted in the death of many soldiers. Despite the conditions, Hussey's cavalry covered the fifty-one miles in twenty-six hours, a remarkable effort, but, in striving to reach their objective in the required time, many horses suffered and had to be destroyed.

Eventually, once he realised that the French were not coming on, Sir John Moore decided to undertake a general withdrawal under cover of darkness. Leaving Hussey and the 7th Hussars to reprise their rôle as rearguard, the remainder of the army marched for Lugo. Those of Hussey's regiment who were still mounted and those whose horses had been put down, all worked together quietly in preparing for their own withdrawal. One problem with which they had to deal, was that they received information that a large enemy force was camped quite near where they lay. Despite that, the task of the 7th was to remain there for, at least, two hours, which they did. Then, Hussey and his men withdrew in relative silence. It was a successful exercise, in the course of which not a single man was lost nor did the French appear to have been aware of any movement. Yet, any euphoria which they might have felt experienced was soon dispelled by the conditions they encountered on the way to Lugo. Following the same route as the main army, the 7th witnessed the distressing spectacles of civilians as well as soldiers literally dying at the roadside. The combination of the weather, fatigue and sickness exacerbated the situation, as did the sight of horses dying in their dozens. To make matters worse, food was very short, camp kettles had been lost and there was no hope of the soldiers putting on fresh clothing.

On 11 January, other than the reserve, the whole army marched into Corunna where the men had believed they would see the transports awaiting them in the bay to take them back to England. However, it was three days later before a ragged cheer went up as the vessels hove into sight. From then on, the rearguard strove to keep the enemy at bay in order to allow the embarkation of the bulk of the British army. Sadly, during the final days of the withdrawal, Sir John Moore died, his shoulder shattered by a cannon ball,[15] and Sir David Baird was wounded very seriously by grapeshot. Eventually, it was the turn of Hussey and his men to board the transports which were left and sail for England. Many of them did so with heavy hearts, because, as a result of a shortage of vessels, by the time they came to board the remaining transports, there was no room for their horses. This was particularly poignant where an animal had lived through the dreadful conditions which had resulted in the death of so many of the mounts belonging to the 7th. With several days in transit to mull over the campaign, once again Hussey attempted to identify the errors which had resulted in another military failure.

Hussey's journal shows that he had firm opinions concerning the conduct of the expedition. There are those who argue that it is wrong to try to analyse combat immediately after the cessation of the action. However, at this distance, and having had the opportunity to read a variety of accounts, it would appear that there is little difference between what might be thought of as the 'mature' commentaries and that of Hussey Vivian, who listed the following errors: 'I cannot help thinking that Corunna should have been defended even to the last extremity'. He went on to argue that there were many physical features favouring the defenders which could have been utilised in defence of the town, whilst the French did not have heavy artillery, which would have been necessary to breach the town's defences.[16]

As for the campaign itself: Hussey saw the ineffective communication system which resulted in Moore's army marching towards the French when Madrid had capitulated, as a key fault.

He claimed that 'bad information, and even the total want of it' had resulted in the making of a poor decisions relating to the advance to the left of Sahagun. The quality of information made available to the military prior to the beginning of the campaign also left a great deal to be desired. 'The poor arrangements of the commissariat' (yet again); the failure to defend the strongest passes in the country, to destroy key bridges, and to halt at Lugo, when the problems caused by the the rapidity of withdrawal, all had an unhelpful influence on the outcome.

His belief that embarking the whole force without attempting to defend Corunna was a poor decision. Indeed, he felt ashamed that the British army had left for home without making a fight of it. On his passage home in the *Barfleur* he had time to consider what he had experienced and, whilst other men, writing after time had passed were to challenge some of Hussey's conclusions, at this distance they appear to be largely apposite. It is interesting that in his analysis, Hussey did not seek to comment on the performance of the cavalry during the Corunna campaign. He might have argued that, despite the faults which he had identified, there was little doubt that in the Corunna actions the British cavalry had established an ascendancy over their French opponents which they were to maintain during the final five years of the Peninsular War.[17] Since he had been involved in many of the Corunna battles, Hussey could have claimed that he had contributed to that success. Furthermore, had he been able to see into the future, he would have seen that his rôle and activities at Waterloo underlined that contribution. The reluctant lawyer who had joined the army for what may be said to be the wrong reasons, had, as a result, found his niche in life.

As the convoy of transports fought their way up the Bay of Biscay they were badly affected by a horrendous storm in which the vessels were tossed around in a maelstrom of a sea. Several ships floundered, and those which reached the English coast put into the first safe haven they could find. Thus it was that survivors were scattered from Land's End to Dover. The men who came ashore were in low spirits, palid, unkempt, and sick, many suffering from with some kind of fever, while sea-sickness added to the misery of many. Hussey and the men who had travelled with him disembarked safely. The civilians who witnessed the homecoming of what appeared to be ragged creatures, must have wondered whether they were the same men whom they had seen marching through their towns.

Hussey, and the men who had travelled with him, disembarked safely. However, on seeking information about the remainder of his regiment, he was distressed to learn that the transport *Dispatch*, carrying three officers, eight NCO's, sixty men and 35 horses, was wrecked on the Manacle Rocks off the Cornish coast. In due course he was to find that other colleagues had also perished in transit and that, of the 751 horses which had left England with the regiment to fight in the Peninsula, only 70 returned. As Alison noted:

'The miserable state of Sir J. Moore's army became the topic of every newspaper along the coast'.[18]

Hussey, himself, having survived again when others around him had succumbed in battle or in transit, might have begun to believe that he was privileged in some way and that he would safely follow his army career through to retirement.

NOTES AND REFERENCES

1. Claud Vivian (ibid.). *Richard Hussey Vivian – a memoir*, p.67.
2. P. J. Haythornthwaite (ibid.). *Wellington's Military Machine*, p.120.
3. The Marquess of Anglesey (ibid.). *A history of the British Cavalry*, Vol 1, p.48.
4. Claud Vivian (op. cit.), p.74.
5. Claud Vivian (op. cit.), p.91.
6. P. J. Haythornthwaite (op. cit.), p.120.
7. Claud Vivian (op. cit.), p.97.
8. Anglesey (op. cit.), p.49.
9. Claud Vivian (op. cit.), p.99.
10. P. J. Haythornthwaite (op. cit.), p.121.
11. Claud Vivian (op. cit.), p.103.
12. The history written by Napier and that of Alison both include a colourful description of this episode. There is no doubt that Napoleon was in the region at the time, while Claud Vivian claims that, subsequently, the Spaniards confirmed that Bonaparte was the soldier on the hill. Claud Vivian (op. cit.), p.103.
13. Claud Vivian (op. cit.), p.105.
14. P. J. Haythornthwaite (op. cit.), p.121.
15. Also see Charles Wolfe (1793-1823) who wrote the epic poem '*The death of Sir John Moore after Corunna*', which became very popular during the Victorian and Edwardian eras. In military circles, Moore was best known for the training programme for infantrymen which he devised, but, presumably he was recognised far more widely. The verse which follows is illustrative of the style adopted by the poet:

No useless coffin enclosed his breast
Not in sheet or in shroud we wound him
But he lay like a warrior taking his rest
With his martial cloke around him.

From the *New Oxford Book of English Verse*,
Helen Gardner, OUP 1972.

16. Claud Vivian (op. cit.), p.123.
17. Anglesey (op. cit.), p.50.
18. Alison (ibid.). *History of Europe*, Vol. VI, p.855.

Chapter Five

Wellesley to Wellington

URING APRIL 1809, Sir Arthur Wellesley landed in Portugal with an army of 23,000 men.[1] He had been appointed Marshal-General of that country, with a remit which gave him complete control over the allied forces there. In reality, however, in the shorter term at least, he could rely only on the British troops. In addition, he was handicapped by the fact that the lessons of Corunna had not been learned; he did not have enough artillery, nor transport and did not have much faith in the effectiveness of the commissariat services. Nevertheless, Wellesley went on the offensive.

At that stage, two French armies were threatening Portugal; Soult, with 24,000 men at his disposal, was at Oporto, and Claude Victor's army of 30,000 was sited adjacent to the fortress of Badajoz. Wellesley's best intelligence suggested that Soult derived comfort from the river Douro which, he believed, protected him on one flank. Wellesley, however, had other ideas and, as a result of a daring ruse which enabled him to land on the French side of the river, a bridgehead was established before the enemy was alerted. Indeed, by the time the French were awake to the attack, Wellesley's men poured through the French camp where they were faced with token resistance, while Soult's men were in full-scale retreat. When bodies were counted, Soult had lost 4,500 men, plus stores and artillery, while only 150 casualties were recorded by Wellesley's army.[2]

By any measure the attack us success. It served as a considerable morale-booster for the British troops, and was another factor in the developing reputation of the British general. No doubt, the soldiers who took part in that attack would have told, perhaps embellished, tales of the young leader they were to call 'Beaky'. At thirty, according to the received wisdom of the times, Wellesley was too young for the command which he held. Not that his men took any notice. They now had an inspiring leader in whom they could place their trust.

Unfortunately, after chasing the French for some ten days, Wellesley had to retire because of shortages of ammunition, food and other supplies: and the initiative was lost. His army had sensed a runaway victory, but the young general knew that he would need to regroup and start afresh. When he was satisfied that his men were ready to take on the French again, he would be doing so having won the profound respect of his troops.

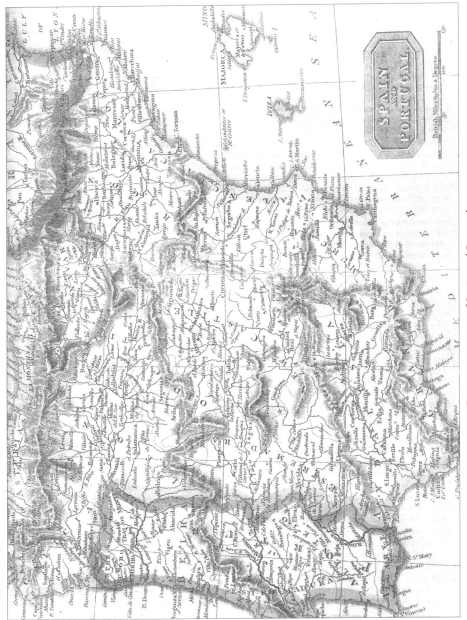

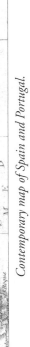

Contemporary map of Spain and Portugal.

Wellesley started planning immediately and, having considered the political as well as the military situation he decided to collaborate with the Spanish general de la Cuesta. The two men met and agreed to attack Claude Victor's army. At the outset the Englishman asked the Spaniard for food and other supplies to satisfy the needs of his men, but they were not forthcoming. Worse, with Victor retreating, there was a window of opportunity open to the allies which Wellesley wished to use before the French reorganised, but much to his chagrin, the Spanish general refused to attack because it was a Sunday. That was a turning-point in the action, and there followed a series of frontal attacks launched by the rejuvenated French, while the British supply lines were under constant threat. Sadly, over 5,000 men were lost in the process of these actions, which took some of the gilt off the Talavera gingerbread.[4] For his part, Wellesley had had his worst fears confirmed regarding the lack of reliability of his allies, which would be a continuing concern for him throughout the campaign.

Back home, despite the setbacks at the later stages of the battle, Talavera was greeted with enthusiasm as a glorious victory. It could be argued that this was the beginning of a trend to lionise the young general, whose popular appeal was growing apace. Whilst it was true that Wellesley had come to general notice as a result of frustrating Napoleon's attempt to invade Mysore from Egypt (1803), the timing of the victory at Talavera, when morale in Britain was at a low ebb, was just what the establishment wanted. Public Relations people, spin doctors and the like may not have been invented at the time, but an astute government and military hierarchy clearly knew how to 'get their message across'. The ennoblement of Sir Arthur Wellesley as Viscount Wellington of Talavera,[5] was an important card to have played in that process. The public welcomed the new Duke of Wellington with open arms. At sea, they had worshipped Nelson. Now, they had a leader on land who would show that 'upstart Napoleon' what the British were made of!

NOTES AND REFERENCES

1. P. J. Haythornthwaite (ibid.). *Wellington's Military Machine*, p.122.
2. Op. cit.
3. P. J. Haythornthwaite (ibid.). *The Armies of Wellington*, p.164.

> 'When . . . first saw Wellington . . . which attracted him, but the shouts of Douro! Douro! from veterans who recognised him'.

> 'Tomkinson overheard two privates of the Light Division referring to their commander as "that long-nosed beggar that licks the French" '.

4. P. J. Haythornthwaite (op. cit.), *Wellington's Military Machine*, p.123.

*   *   *

Given Hussey's penchant for analysis, there is little doubt that he would have questioned his colleagues who had taken part in the battle at Talavera so as to learn from what happened there. He was aware that Wellington was cautious about cavalry men, particularly when they were caught up in the excitement of the charge. The fundamental mistake which had been made during the action put that distrust into context. It seemed that, towards the end of the battle, the 23rd Light Dragoons and the 1st German Hussars advanced at a trot over ground which had, running across its breadth, a hidden water course. While still some way off the enemy position they broke into a canter, at which pace they were charging when they came upon the obstacle. Confusion reigned, then, as horses and men clattered to the ground. As the officers tried to regain control, the ragged group found themselves in two parties, one facing a solid French infantry square, whilst the other was outnumbered 5-1 by Chausseurs. The outcome was that the regiment lost 207 men and 22 horses – almost half its strength. It was a far too costly an outcome for whatever gains had been made. Hussey must have noted the lessons to be learned about impetuosity, while it is probable that Wellington's view of cavalry would have been reinforced by the incident.

See The Marquess of Anglesey, *A History of the British Cavalry*, Vol. 1, p.50.

5. Wellesley was gazetted as the Duke of Wellington on 3 May 1814.

Chapter Six

The Return of the Tyrant

FOLLOWING THE FIRST abdication of Napoleon (April 1814) and his banishment to the island of Elba, Wellington's victorious Peninsular Army was disbanded. The prospect of peace after many years of war was welcomed all over Europe. In Britain, the end of hostilities was greeted even more warmly, particularly by the Treasury. Peace, its officials reasoned, would not only significantly reduce the costs generated by the country's large army, but Britain would also benefit from not being required to pay significant sums of money to subsidise the armies of several of its allies. Even Wellington was caught up in, what today would be called, 'downsizing', for without such an army, the rôle of Commander-in-Chief would be diminished. Recognising this, the British cabinet discussed ways in which the Duke's talents might be best used for the good of the nation. Their solution was to create a new post; that of British Ambassador to France.

In the meantime, after recovering from his wound, Hussey Vivian was promoted to the rank of Major-General, and appointed to command the Sussex Military District. In accepting this post, Hussey was obliged to sever his connection with the Hussars, a parting which was marked by his brother officers making a presentation to him 'of plate worth 250 guineas'.[1] He was also knighted, which meant that he then became Major-General Sir Richard Hussey Vivian. He was looking forward to his new rôle but, unbeknown to him, circumstances were to change his best-laid plans. Thus it was that on 16 April he found himself in Brussels, having responded to an urgent call of duty from the Duke of Wellington. He was the first soldier of the rank of general to do so. Clearly, Hussey's statement about not unsheathing his sword again, had been overtaken by this call to arms. When duty called, Hussey responded.

The Iron Duke was similarly placed, in that he had taken up his ambassadorial rôle with considerable enthusiasm. Almost immediately, he was involved with the Foreign Secretary, Viscount Castlereagh, in a congress of the allied nations, which was then in session at Paris (May 1814), its purpose being to agree on territorial boundaries following Napoleon's defeat. To this end, Castlereagh had a clear objective which he was working to achieve. He wanted to persuade the representatives of the interested countries to agree to a pan-European solution to the problems raised by the differing expectations of the member states. Castlereagh, representing Britain, the only country not to be seeking territorial gains, was regarded as generally neutral. Consequently, together with Wellington, his was a formidable figure in the discussions. He wanted to ensure that individual countries did not reach agreements with others which were divisive in the broader scheme of things. By the end of the Paris meetings, Castlereagh had only succeeded in getting two countries to agree to his plan. This resulted in a second congress being arranged, this time in Vienna (Autumn 1814). Not that there was any expectation that concord would be achieved at that venue. Indeed, it was not until November 1815 that the final settlement was signed though, as Petrie noted, that agreement was to last for 45 years.[2]

While the Foreign Secretary was absorbed in his dealings with other nations around the world, Wellington proceeded on another mission. The Duke had an outstanding reputation in the Peninsula, and the allies believed that he could assist in solving a difficult problem in Spain. There, King Ferdinand VII had gone back to his own country after being incarcerated in France from the time when Napoleon had usurped the Spanish throne and replaced Ferdinand with his own brother. On his return, the king was in a foul mood, for he found that some of his subjects wished to arrange matters in a more liberal way. The view of the European states was that, if the arguments escalated, there was a real danger of a civil war breaking out in the Peninsula. Given Wellington's fame and reputation amongst the Spanish, it was generally agreed that he was the man who, in acting as a mediator, had the best chance of influencing the situation so as to avoid such a conflict. In only twelve days he made considerable progress in meeting his objective. Other events then took centre-stage and the Spanish question was shelved *pro tem.*

For Castlereagh, the Vienna Congress started badly. Following the end of the Paris discussions and the beginning of those at Vienna, tacit behind-the-scenes agreements had evolved to a stage where the problems associated with uniting the delegates seemed insurmountable.[3] Furthermore, others were watching developments, and there was hostility between the two great Germanic powers, Austria and Prussia. At one stage it looked as though the British Foreign Secretary had lost control of the discussions, but he stuck to his task doggedly. Fighting back, he took on the rôle of blunt spokesman for the moderates in discussions with the Russians over Poland. In the early months of 1815, diplomatic exchanges were continuing, with seemingly little progress being made, but the news of the return of Napoleon focused minds. The delegates accepted that, if they wished to defeat Bonaparte, they would need to work together, and Castlereagh took the opportunity to emphasise to each member state the importance of such an alliance. With Napoleon free and threatening, they might have had in mind the old saw, 'United we stand, divided we fall'.

Napoleon had landed on 1 March 1815 near Cannes. It was reported that he had with him his staff and an army of 1,200.[4] Wellington must have been cursing his luck for, had he even dreamed that Napoleon might return, perhaps he could have postponed the break-up of his Peninsular army. The experience and loyalty of these men would have made a considerably greater contribution to Wellington's cause, for these soldiers were veterans of many campaigns. More importantly, they knew the way he approached battles, they trusted him, and whilst he was not popular in the broad sense, there was a morale-boosting bond between 'Beaky' and them all.

On learning of Bonaparte's re-emergence, and the mass-desertions to his side of men who had joined the royalist army while the Tyrant was imprisoned on Elba, Wellington made his way north to the Netherlands. There he assumed command of the Belgian, Dutch, Prussian, and British forces. Immediately on arrival at Brussels he sought information as to what British troops and equipment were in the area, and, also, in Britain. Particularly, he wanted to know which senior officers were available to him. The exercise was repeated with the allied armies. The first appointment was Wellington's second-in-command, Lord Uxbridge, who was to lead the cavalry in the battle, and then Major-General Sir Richard Hussey Vivian, the first soldier of the rank of General to respond. At Waterloo, Hussey was to lead one of the three brigades of cavalry.

When Hussey arrived in Belgium on 16 April 1815, he found himself caught up in a round of social as well as military engagements. In the days which followed he dined on different evenings with Wellington, the Duke of Richmond, the Paymaster General, and his friend, Lord Uxbridge. He also attended a cricket match and a horse racing meeting. In addition, with two other officers and Uxbridge, he set out in the second-in-command's carriage, to inspect the work which was being undertaken by the Sappers to reinforce the defensive fortifications which helped to protect Brussels. In turn, he attended, or participated in several troop reviews, which enabled him to get to know another group of officers.

Whilst Napoleon, largely unopposed, was making his way through France, Louis XVIII was making public pronouncements to the effect that those who were afraid should leave at once. In private, however, he, himself was ready to flee at a moment's notice, for his valuables were packed and ready; the prospect of the guillotine being less than attractive to him. Meantime, Wellington maintained his *sang froid* to the extent that he and his senior officers were attending a ball given by the Duchess of Richmond, when he was informed that Bonaparte had pushed back the Prussians near Quartre Bras.

On hearing the news, the Duke was reported as having said: 'Napoleon has humbugged me, by God'. Unlike Drake, who had insisted on finishing his game of bowls, Wellington's officers had to hasten back to their quarters, and proceed to the places and positions to which they had been allocated. With torrential rain falling, poor roads on which to travel, and the extent of the distances involved (some had to travel forty miles) the officers must have wondered about the quality of the intelligence upon which they had based their decision-making. Napoleon had caught them 'on the hop'.

NOTES AND REFERENCES

1. W. H. Tregelles (ibid.). *Some Cornish Worthies*, Vol II (1894), p.352.
2. Quoted in Jac Weller (ibid.). *Wellington at Waterloo*. New edition (1992), p.11.
3. The discordance carried over from the Paris congress caused Castlereagh and Wellington many difficulties. Part of the problem was of the Foreign Secretary's own making, for he disregarded his own 'rules' for the congress by involving France in a secret pact with Britain and Austria. The purpose of this grouping was to block Russian and Prussian ambitions with respect to their territorial ambitions regarding Poland and Saxony. Castlereagh was, still, pursuing his pan European ambition.
4. See Lt. Colonel Gurwood (ibid.). *The dispatches of Wellington*, XII, 266 (1837-8).

Chapter Seven

À bas le Tyran

D URING AUGUST 1813, military developments in the Iberian Peninsula were such that Wellington called for reinforcements. Among those who responded to that call was Colonel Hussey Vivian who, with his regiment, was ordered to proceed to Bilbao where he was to join with the Duke of Wellington's army. Hussey, his men their horses and equipment, set sail in the middle of the month in a convoy of transport vessels. In view of what had happened in the Peninsula, it was appropriate that Colonel Hussey travelled aboard the *Lord Wellington*. Fortunately, the weather was fine, and Hussey and the bulk of the 'non-sailors' in his party completed a sea voyage for the first time without being sick. Thus it was that he and his troops were in good spirits when they disembarked in the sunshine at their destination. It was a good start!

After ensuring that his regiment and horses were properly billeted, Hussey went to inspect his own accommodation, and there is no doubt that he was delighted with what he found. His description of what he called his 'mansion' speaks volumes about his enthusiasm for the place:

> Its situation is beautiful . . . on the river in the midst of magnificent mountains, and in peace . . . I have no doubt that it is a delightful residence . . . The Alemada on which my mansion stands is near the bank of the river, and is planted around with trees'.[1]

In many respects, his situation was quite different from that which he had experienced the first time he had arrived at the Peninsula. Furthermore, there was the comforting fact that two servants had been made available to him; a general factotum, and a cook/housekeeper. Nonetheless, given his temperament, it was not surprising that, after the initial enjoyment of living in such an idyllic place, he began to wonder about his orders. It was clear to him that the campaign in which he was to be embroiled was a very important element in the drive to free Europe of the menace of Napoleon. That being so, the attractions of his mansion could not entirely compensate for the lack of contact from the his superior officers. He complained that he 'had not heard a syllable from anyone . . . and, I seldom see a paper, even'. Then, presumably to re-assure his wife about his safety in the months ahead, he gave it as his opinion that, 'There will not be much fighting in this campaign'. By then, as an experienced army officer, he must have realised that the explosive potential of a campaign where Wellington and Napoleon were to oppose each other, was unlikely to be a riskless process. It would appear that he wished to shield his wife from this truth.

In the meantime, it was evident that he was still ambitious. For example, in the same letter he said that he had heard that a brigade colonel was seriously ill and, if that was true, it was probable that the man would be sent home. Were that to happen, he felt that there was a good chance that he would receive promotion and be given command of a brigade. As he put it, 'I do not like leaving the 7th, but the emoluments of a brigade are not to be refused'.[2]

Eventually, after what seemed to Hussey to be a very long time, he was summoned to Wellington's headquarters. In the interim, whilst awaiting developments, he had attempted to analyse the military situation. Consequently, he felt that, given the opportunity, he should be able to show the Duke that he had a sound grasp of the military scenario. On arrival, he found that he was invited to dine with Lieutenant-General Sir Stapleton-Cotton, whom he described subsequently as being 'excessively civil and kind'. Hussey also reported that, whilst his host told him that he did not have a brigadeship to offer, the implication was that one would be forthcoming in the not too distant future. At least, that was how Hussey interpreted the various comments which had been made.

As has been suggested earlier, he saw the welfare of his troops as being an extremely important part of his task as a leader of men; an ethic which has been at the heart of the rôle of the British army officer for centuries. A journal entry following a visit to an old friend exemplifies one aspect of this. During discussion over dinner, Hussey had been briefed in some detail about key actions. San Sebastian was one town which he had passed through, and his journal note could be summed-up as describing the place as 'being in a horrible state'. He learned that the assault, which had wrenched control of the citadel from the French, had cost the lives of more than 2,000 men. It gave him much to think about for, in the past, he had taken himself to task regarding his concerns for humanity. The incident where the opportunity to shoot at Napoleon was missed was an example. Yet, in spite of his personal feelings, his primary maxim as a soldier never wavered, 'Duty' was paramount.

When Hussey finally met Wellington, he was disappointed to find that the 'audience' did not develop as he had hoped. 'The great Lord', as he described the Duke, 'had but made his bow and said very little'. The following day, as Hussey made his way back to Bilbao, he had plenty of time to ponder on this situation, although he did not come to any firm conclusions. As so often happens, what appears to be a problem on one day is put into the right context on subsequent days. It was no different for Hussey. Having arrived at Bilbao, he found his orders

'The Warrior of the West' leads his men into battle.

A Hussar of the 6th Light Dragoons assessing the position in battle.

A corporal and a sergeant of the 7th or 'Queen's Own' Light Dragoons.

A corporal and two officers of the 7th or 'Queen's Own' Light Dragoons (Hussars).

Soldiers of the French 4th regiment plus a Hussar.
Left to right: a Grenadier, an Infantryman and a Hussar.

awaiting him. Against a backcloth of a strong rumour that Wellington was planning to cross the border into France, Hussey learned that the 7th were required to march to Tafalla to join with the Hussar Brigade, under Lord Edward Somerset. The die was cast.

While there was never any question that he regarded his orders as a clear call to duty to which he would respond accordingly, it is interesting to note that, in a letter to his wife, written before he became involved in action, he expressed his feelings more freely than on similar occasions in the past. He wrote of his love for his family, his concerns about being separated from, and how much he missed being with them. His justification for being where he was, was simply that, 'My prospects are my profession. If I am to get a regiment or a staff appointment, I must do my duty now'.[3] Of such complexities are heroes made.

In order to open a route through the Pyrenees, Wellington had concluded that he would need to take control of both the fortified towns which stood in his way. His opponent, Soult, was, of course, doing all he could to hamper the British advance which, given the determination of both men to achieve their objectives, resulted in fighting of an unusually ferocious kind. Wellington, indeed, is reported as having said 'I never saw such fighting as we have had here . . . the battle of the 28th was fair bludgeon work'.[4]

Following the fall of Pampeluna, the second fortified town in Wellington's way, Hussey and his men were ordered to march to Salines de Pampeluna and Noain, following which they were to advance to Arraix and St. Estevan, and then proceed into France by the Maya pass. The time objectives involved in these marches were very demanding. Hussey called them 'forced marches' and recorded the loss of horses and mules. Fortunately, near St. Estevan they were ordered to halt, and the relieved Hussey was grateful. As he put it:

> 'I say "Thank God", because another such a day's march as we had yesterday, and the regiment would have been *hors de combat*'.[5]

He went on to describe the poor condition of the roads and mountain paths which they had to climb *en route* to their destination. He said that the 'worst goat path in Wales is a garden walk compared to some of them'.[6] In addition, there was precious little in the way of food to be gathered in. There was also the question of fatigue, for he and his troops, had been in the saddle from seven in the morning until six in the evening and, in that time they had covered just nine miles. Had these soldiers been required to fight at this point, it would have been a Herculean task for them. Apart from anything else, twenty horses had lost shoes, and all of them were tired. This situation forced Hussey to leave half his force behind him as he advanced to his next objective. Fortunately, by the time new orders had arrived, the brigade was virtually complete and proceeded to a place called Vera. The 7th

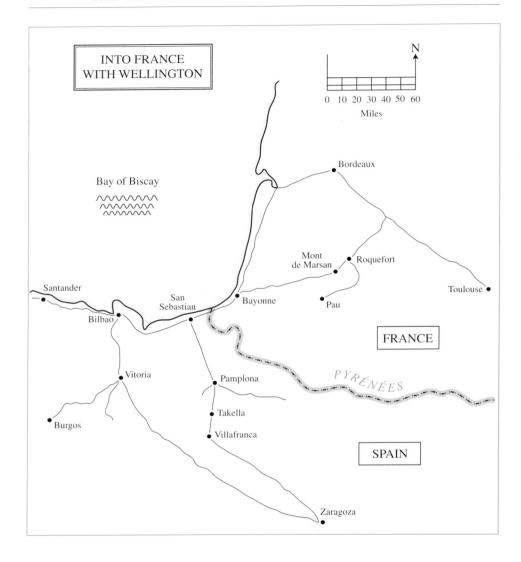

INTO FRANCE
WITH WELLINGTON

N

0 10 20 30 40 50 60
Miles

Bordeaux

Bay of Biscay

Mont
de Marsan

Roquefort

Santander

San
Sebastian

Bayonne

Toulouse

Pau

FRANCE

Bilbao

Vitoria

Pamplona

P Y R É N É E S

Burgos

Takella

Villafranca

SPAIN

Zaragoza

arrived there to find that there were still considerable problems with supplies. Too
many armies, it seemed, had been living off the land. Later, the 7th, it was said,
had contributed towards Wellington's victory, but the general feeling among Hussey's
force was that they could have done better had they not been faced with a drastic
lack of supplies, and had been given the chance to 'recharge their batteries'.

As for Hussey Vivian himself, he was delighted to be learn that he had won the
promotion he had set his mind on achieving. From that point on he could use the
title Brigadier. Although, in a letter to his wife he pointed out that he would receive
about 28s. per day, but was expected to keep up with his 'brother brigadiers'.
Among other things, this involved buying Lord Waldegrave's canteen of cutlery for

£200 and selling his own for £60 or £70.[7] No one in the network seemed to be called 'Jones', but the environment within which such transactions occurred were of a kind which might have spawned the well-known saying 'keeping up with . . .' The modern reader may find it rather curious that, in the middle of a war, the 'officers and gentlemen' were still concerned about status and position in a societal sense. But then, it is as difficult for that reader to understand the attitudes and structures of society from which these men emerged.

After the battle of Nivelle, Wellington was concerned about the size of the area in which his armies were confined. The Duke would have preferred to break out and attack the enemy rather than co-exist as was the pattern at that time. It was a case of 'rain stopped battle', for torrential downpour after downpour resulted in swollen rivers and acres of mud. Such was the scale of the problem that it was the beginning of December before Wellington was prepared to attack the French again.

It was during the lull between actions that Hussey took up his new appointment, where he was to command the cavalry between Ustarits and Cambo on the river Nive. His quarters were at Laressore in the Chateau de San Martin and, in a letter to his wife, he sang its praises. 'You can have no conception of anything more magnificently beautiful than the situation of my chateau . . . .'. He explained that the chateau was quite near to the banks of the river Nive, which was narrow. On the opposite bank the French were encamped. And, during the period of 'disengagement' the enemy and the British had come to an agreement not to fire on each other. General Pringle, who commanded an infantry brigade had no doubt about the safety of the arrangements.

Consequently, social meetings were set up by officers on both sides. Strange as it may seem today's reader, these officers were simply doing what they were accustomed to as gentlemen in civilian life. Although the truce had been appreciated by British and French officers alike, the arrangement would necessarily be of only short duration.

War recommenced and, in thick fog, following a series of feints, attacks and counter-attacks, Soult sent his cavalry to engage that of Sir S. Cotton and Hussey Vivian. During one of these engagements, Hussey was involved in an action which resulted in controversy several years later. Napier, a major figure in the Military History field, made the first of several attacks on Hussey in which he charged the Cornishman with poor judgment of a situation to the detriment of some soldiers in his brigade. Napier's version of the events (written some time later) had it that:

> 'Colonel Vivian, who commanded there, immediately ordered Major Brotherton to charge with the 14th Dragoons across the bridge; but it was an ill-judged order . . . Only two men and one subaltern passed the bridge . . . Vivian then, seeing his error, charged with his whole brigade to rescue them, yet in vain'.[8]

Not surprisingly, Hussey Vivian's biographer, would have felt unwilling to accept what amounted to a slur on his forebear's honour, and, as a result, set in motion a search from which the two versions of the action might be compared in an objective light. Napier's informant, one Major W. Brotherton, subsequently admitted that he was 'in some measure wrong' in what had been written. According to the *Royal United Service Journal,*[9] there was a promise made to put the matter right in any future editions of his work. Since some of the 'mud thrown' at the time of the original publication would have 'stuck', this was a less than satisfactory outcome for Hussey. Furthermore, for whatever reason, Napier was critical of Hussey Vivian on several other occasions. As will be seen later in this text, given the tone of these comments, it rather suggests that Napier did not like Hussey.

During the battle which ensued, at one point one of the brigades under Hussey's command was sent elsewhere, leaving him with only the 14th Hussars. Since he was facing two brigades of enemy cavalry, and had been told to contain them, he admitted in a letter home that he had been 'worried and harassed by the task'. However, his claim that he had not undressed for four days, seems like an overstatement. Though, given the dreadful conditions (they were covered with mud from head to foot), whilst being without their baggage, it might have seemed like that.

During mid-December rumours were circulating to the effect that the allied armies, including those of Russia, Prussia and Austria were combining to march into France. According to this gossip, Napoleon was out of favour with the French people. He had, by then, washed his hands of Spain and Portugal, while Soult and Foy must have been feeling vulnerable. Foy had failed to complete the building of a fortified bridge across the river at Urt. Such failure, of course reflected badly on Soult, his commanding officer.

Hussey's concerns were more localised, Alten was going home and it was the opinion of the staff that Hussey should take over from him. His attempt to decline on the grounds that he was happy where he was did not alter the situation. There was another unhappy matter, too, with which Hussey had to deal. He had received, in reply to his letter to the 7th, written on taking leave of that regiment, what he called an abominably cold reply. According to Hussey, his own letter had been dictated from the heart, and 'I spoke of my feelings towards the regiment'. From his comments upon the situation, it is clear that he was very disappointed not to get a similarly warm letter in return.[10]

On the first day of January, 1814, Hussey took command of his brigade, which comprised the 18th Hussars, and the German Hussars. Unfortunately, just days before his transfer was complete, the 18th blotted their collective copybook when they became involved in a hectic skirmish. The Spanish who were with them withdrew, but did not inform the commander of the party, Major Hughes. One result of this action was that the cavalry were wrong-footed, one captain being killed and two other officers wounded.

This was hardly helpful, for in Wellington's eyes there were already question marks against the 18th, which were said to have stemmed from the behaviour of the regiment in plundering following the battle of Vitoria. To add to Hussey's woe, having established himself in attractive quarters, he was, as he put it, 'turned-out' by General Fane. It hardly boded well for Hussey's future with the 18th. Four days later, however, he found that he had his old regiment, the 7th, under his command. He took the opportunity to invite four of his old colleagues to dinner, following which he understood a little more about the background to the 'cold' letter which he had received. Even so, it was something which he found difficult to erase from his mind. The 7th had been, as it were, his 'baby' and, in all sincerity, the letter which had been sent to him had come as a disappointment which he found difficult to understand. Nonetheless, his dinner companions had been charming and all parties had enjoyed the evening, food and conversation. He had appreciated the company, and their friendly faces had helped him to come to terms with the problem letter. Obviously, he would need to develop new networks, but after so many years, by and large, with the same people, the task was far from simple.

Whilst Wellington still wished to advance into France, the weather was not favourable. Rain had swollen the rivers and mud made it difficult to move people, supplies and, particularly, artillery. The Duke was also short of troops. Meanwhile, the paradoxical arrangements between British officers and their French counterparts were widespread. Hussey, in a letter to his brother, gave as an example a morning when, at half past four, he was awakened by firing. He galloped down to the front and found that 150 French had attacked a hill on their side of the river on which Hussey had about twenty men. By the time Hussey Vivian arrived, the British had been driven beyond the river. With the firing still continuing, he went to the river bank and 'halloaed to the French to cease firing and send an officer to me'. This resulted in one of D'Armagnac's ADC's appearing. The officers gave the necessary orders to their respective men and then talked together for half an hour.

With rumours circulating on both banks of the river that peace would be made before many months had passed, Hussey's view was that he favoured a 'good peace', by which he meant one which was honourable and liberal to all parties. Hussey believed that it would not do 'to screw anyone too tight; the consequence would be a renewal of the war on the first opportunity'. It was his final sentence, however, which gave a clear signal as to his innermost thoughts. He wrote: 'for my part, if I once sheathe the sword I do not wish to unsheathe it'. This sentence provides us with a better understanding of the inner Hussey Vivian. It suggests, among other things, that he was concerned about his 'luck' on the battlefield. He had served through several campaigns during which some of his friends were killed, and, as he got older their number increased. He had, also, challenged his own position regarding his views on humanitarian issues. Yet, he remained a professional soldier with an unimpeachable belief in doing his duty.

Despite those concerns and the strength of the rumours (which might, of course, very well be less than accurate) on the 21st of January 1814 Hussey instructed his wife to send him: 'My two ADC's coats, six shirts, four pairs of net pantaloon drawers, four under-waistcoats, twelve pairs of half stockings (thin worsted), six black ties, six white waistcoats I have at home, and a half a dozen pairs of the nankeen overalls and white trousers, some of each for summer wear'. There was a rider, however; 'send nothing till peace or war is decided'.[11]

Six days later, in his next letter he revealed his financial concerns. Presumably responding to a question about further promotion to Major-General, he replied that he did not expect a brevet at that time because of the consequences if peace was achieved. He went on to argue that if there was peace he would be worse off, for he would lose his ADC's pay, would have to 'come off the staff', would find it difficult to gain employment in England and did not wish to go to the East or West Indies.

Then, after what appeared like an age during which relatively friendly relationships with the French had been the norm, warfare recommenced. Hussey and his men were on the march again. His orders were clear, and by 25 February, his brigade had made considerable progress, without meeting any serious opposition. The weather was fine and the going firmer, all rivers were fordable and roads passable. On that day they had marched from Bastide de Berne to Sorbe, Cassabe and Carivo, all villages on the banks of the Gave d'Oloron. Hussey's spirits were lifted by the speed of the advance. If nothing else, the activities in which he and his men were engaged did not allow him to dwell upon his personal concerns. He was extremely pleased, too, with his quarters, for he was housed in 'a capital chateau, belonging to the ancient Comte de Berieux at Cassabre'. Hussey and his colleagues were provided with every comfort whilst they were there, and their collective opinion was that they thought the ambience of the place was reminiscent of a 'good old English Nobleman's house'.[12] Clearly, Hussey enjoyed his creature comforts.

The next day, Hussey led his men (four squadrons) across the Gave de Pau at Hointon. After the static situation at Laressore he found this to be exhilarating, a sensation which was enhanced by the sighting of a highway which, he thought, 'is more admirable than any road I ever beheld'. On arrival, at what had been the French side, Hussey learned that there was a party of enemy cavalry at a village called Puyoo, and he determined to take them on. Selecting twenty well-mounted men to augment the patrol (which comprised a similar number) he charged the French. At this, the enemy turned tail and were not caught until they had run about two miles. After a short action, the British took six prisoners without the loss of one man. Unfortunately, by then most of the horses were blown, and Hussey could not press home his advantage. In addition, he had experienced a challenging one-to-one situation during which he had saved himself by 'cutting the man at the elbow', and disarming him in the process. At that time, the incident did not seem to have been important in terms of the overall situation. Later, however, it was found to have been significant. The officer in charge of the French cavalry group had failed to report the incident. According to Napier, that omission 'enabled Beresford to make the movements he did in safety', when otherwise he would have been 'assailed by at least two-thirds of the French army'.[13]

There followed developments in many sections of the front which were beneficial to Wellington's cause. Whilst they had achieved much, the British found that the enemy was established in prepared positions on heights covering Orthez. Not withstanding this, the Duke's men marched to attack. After about three hours of very severe fighting, the enemy began to give way at every point, although they fought on, retiring from position to prepared position. Post-battle analysis showed that the victory had cost the lives of some 3,000 Allied troops. The enemy, however, had lost even more and, in his retreat, Soult abandoned his magazines at Mont de Marsan, which prompted Wellington to detach Beresford and Hussey Vivian and their cavalry divisions to secure the stores. Such was Hussey's contribution to the victory at Orthez that, after the action, he was awarded a clasp to his gold Peninsular Medal following the approbation of Sir W. Beresford.

Mont de Marsan was the next town in which Hussey and his men were quartered. Once again, the brigadier found very comfortable facilities and a pleasant host, which was just as well, for the weather was dreadful. Indeed, Hussey believed it to be the worst he had ever experienced, hail, rain, snow, thunder, lightning, and wind all in the same day. He was in the process of describing the town and his landlord, M. Barrière, who 'has supplied me with excellent claret and brandy, gratis', when he had to stop writing, having been ordered to march immediately.

Intelligence suggested that the enemy had taken up a given position, but before they arrived there, Hussey was instructed to halt and arrange accommodation for the men and horses. Unfortunately, there was not a great deal anyone could do, for they were in the middle of a pine forest and, it was not until past midnight that a 'wretched hovel' was found and pressed into service as his headquarters. Happily, conditions improved somewhat by the next day and, although covered with mud, the brigade continued marching towards Villeneuve. On arrival there, once again no enemy troops were to be found. Hussey's view was that they should strike for Bordeaux, but, whilst awaiting orders to that effect, patrols from the brigade scoured the country for the enemy. At dawn on the next day, the march took them first to Langon and subsequently to Castres, whence they set out for Bordeaux, early on the morning of March 12.

At about 8 o'clock, Hussey's advanced patrol reported that 600 infantry and 150 cavalry had crossed the Garonne six hours earlier, and that no one would offer resistance. Hussey, with a small party, proceeded into the town where he found an armed guard of around a hundred drawn up awaiting the arrival of the British. As Hussey put it: 'I rode quietly up to their commanding officer and from him learnt that no opposition was intended'.[14] It was then agreed that a formal ceremony would take place, following which Marshal Beresford would enter the town on behalf of Lord Wellington. Presumably, as a result of his experience as ADC in the service of the Prince Regent, Hussey showed that he was aware of diplomatic issues. When reporting to Beresford about the situation he urged that consideration should be given to the mayor's intention to hoist the white flag and for the population to wear white cockades. Hussey's was concerned about the possible interpretation that might be placed on such actions. He feared that some people would see this as a symbolic 'surrender', imposed upon Bordeaux at the insistence of the British army. Both Beresford and Hussey were, by then, aware of the diplomatic moves which were taking place at that time with the objective of ending the war and removing Napoleon from his position of power. Beresford saw the relevance of the argument and it was arranged for the ceremony to take place without involving the people of Bordeaux in donning the symbols of defeat. Hussey took pains to ensure that everyone involved understood and agreed with the suggested approach, but in the event local sentiments could not be satisfied.

On the day when the ceremony took place Marshal Beresford announced that the British were entering the town as friends and without bloodshed. Furthermore, should the current negotiations break down and Napoleon be able to regain his powerful control, then Britain would support the town in every way possible. At first, the mayor's response was received in relative silence but, when he discarded his tricolour sash and replaced it and the favour in his hat with white alternatives, there was a great roar and shouts of 'À bas le tyran!' Whilst the mayor had persisted with his wish to wear white, his speech made it clear that it represented the wishes of the people of Bordeaux.

Following the ceremony, Hussey and the Marshal dined and then went to the theatre together. Hussey devoted the next day to familiarising himself with the town, and in a letter to his wife he described it as: 'a residence where you can have every luxury the world affords, and at about one-fourth of the price you can procure them elsewhere'. He occupied the next two days in a similar way and dined again with Beresford, this time in the company of the Duc d'Angouleme. He was enjoying his sojourn in Bordeaux, but, late that evening, he received orders to march at daybreak to Barsac and then, by forced marches, make contact with Wellington's army.

It was on the 18 March that he wrote, briefly, of a tremendous march of 8 leagues which brought him to Roquefort, and had 'knocked up all our baggage animals'.[15] The next day was no better, for they travelled another 7 leagues. In all, over four days, Hussey and his men marched over 32 leagues, some of which was through soft sand which reached the fetlocks of the horses. By any measure it was hard going.

By the 24th, following inclement weather, shortages of food and fodder and little in the way of accommodation, the state of many of his men was pitiable. Conditions had improved little on arrival at Colomien four days later, when engineers failed in their attempt to throw a pontoon across the Garonne. This caused Wellington to move the bulk of his army to the right, leaving Hussey's brigade and that of the Hussars to watch developments on the roads to Auch and Boulogne.

At the time, Hussey had no way of knowing that the bridge work had not been completed and, on observing French troops in front beginning to withdraw, he assumed that this was because of British troops had crossed the intended bridge. Thus it was that Hussey, espying the 10th Chasseurs and some infantry along a road which led to the environs of the town, gave chase. *En route* the brigade came under fire from five cannons which formed a battery designed to enfilade the road. Seeing the effect of that, he ordered his men to turn about and withdraw. His losses were minimal, but the benefits of the movement became apparent later, for the brigade was able to take up an excellent position overlooking Toulouse. Meantime the whole Allied army was moving up on the town, but the conditions were deplorable. Hussey, writing to his wife, described the men as being 'in rags' and 'most of the infantry are without shoes. Their sufferings are dreadful'.[16]

On 3 April, Wellington ordered Hussey to join with him and Marshal Beresford in a reconnaissance along the river. Hussey assumed that, once a decision was made regarding the crossing point, his cavalry were to be involved. After a long ride and much deliberation, it was decided that a pontoon would be laid across the river at 2 o'clock on the following morning. The bridge was to be erected at a site near Grenade. Hussey noted that enemy pickets were based on both sides of the river which, he reasoned, would result in what he termed 'hot work'. The plan was for the 4th Division to be in the van, followed closely by Hussey's brigade. Before he snatched a few hours' sleep that night, Hussey wrote a short letter to his wife, from which it is apparent that fears for his own mortality were still very real for him, if only at the back of his mind. He wrote:

> 'My brigade of cavalry follows the 4th, which goes first: So the devil is in it if I do not get a hit at gentlemen tomorrow. I have always been in luck and got off well and so, please God, I mean to do'.[17]

At first, the pontoon worked well, three brigades of cavalry crossing along with three divisions of infantry, but subsequently the depth of the water and the rate of its flow damaged the bridge so much that it could not be used where it was. A new site had to be found for the crossing. One consequence of this was that the Light Division, the Spaniards, and the Heavy Germans were unable to follow. At the time, however, Hussey was unaware of that fact. Initially, it looked as if Soult was about to attack the detachments of Wellington's army which had crossed the river and were cut off, but it proved not to be so. Hussey, noting the dishevelled, miserable looking army, 'drenched to the skin and up to their knees in mud', was heartened by the effect on these same men of the bands playing 'British Grenadiers'. Eventually, when he learned about the bridging problem, Hussey recorded in his journal:

'We have just 10,700 bayonets and 2,200 swords. If Soult does not take advantage of this opportunity and attack us he is not worth his salt'.[18]

It was not an encouraging scenario, but his response was defiant. Whether it resulted from bravado, a bout of positive thinking or some other stimulant, in addressing his journal again, he gave it as his opinion:

'However, if he does, he will get thrashed; for my firm belief is that the three divisions here would beat his whole army'.

Because that army was at least double the strength of the British units which had crossed, it was a reasonable conclusion to draw that Soult must have recognised the opportunity which was open to him. Nonetheless, whether it was because of the torrential rain during the night, or the recognition that diplomatic negotiations were taking place at a high level in Paris, Soult did not attack.

Given that Napoleon abdicated on 6 April 1814, it might have been assumed that this would have brought an end to warfare at that time, since further military action was not necessary. Wellington, however, appears not to have received that information, and with his army together again on the same side of the river, on the 8 April he advanced towards Toulouse. It was during that march that, at one point, the river Ers separated the two armies. Wishing to cross in order to engage the enemy and without pontoons, it was essential that at least one of the stone bridges which spanned the river be secured. Initially, neither side appeared to have the conviction to attack the other. In the end each army sounded the charge at the same time, but the British cavalry proved sharper than the enemy. Their momentum gave them advantage and, during a ferocious action, the bridge was secured by Vivian's Hussars. Unfortunately, after ordering the charge, Hussey was wounded by a shot from a dismounted rifleman and was unable to lead his brigade in attaining the objective.[19]

Wellington's despatch regarding the event outlines the action as it unfolded. He wrote:

'. . . the 18th Hussars under the immediate command of Colonel Vivian had the opportunity of making a most gallant attack upon a superior body of the enemy's cavalry, which they drove through the village of Croix d'Orade and took about 100 prisoners and gave us possession of an important bridge over the Ers . . . Colonel Vivian was unfortunately wounded upon this occasion and I am afraid I shall lose his services for some time'.[20]

Several years later, Colonel Napier showed, once again, that he was less than impartial when it came to Hussey Vivian. He took the trouble to point out that Vivian had been wounded before the charge and that credit for its execution was due to another officer. Wellington's despatch, immediately after the action, and Sir S. Cotton in Cavalry Orders around the same time, took a different view. It is interesting to note that several of these issues are discussed by Claud Vivian, the author of a biography of his grandfather's life. Cynics might query whether the grandson would have been able to write objectively about his famous forebear. However, in his book he raises several of these issues (when he might well have ignored them) and makes a genuine effort to detail them in a careful and considered fashion. The reader may care to weigh the arguments put forward puts forward by Napier, along with those advanced by his biographer, in the light with the character of Hussey Vivian portrayed in this volume.

Two pieces of evidence which Claud Vivian introduced may help in this comparison. Whatever Colonel Napier or any other observer said or wrote about the Cornish hero, it is difficult to refute the common thread which runs through both items. First, following the day of the action referred to in Wellington's despatch, Hussey Vivian received a letter from the officers of the 18th Hussars. It was something of a eulogy and, whilst the sentences are rather complicated, appears to be the sincere reaction of his fellow officers to his wounding.

> Dear Sir, – In proportion to the gratitude we entertain for the occasion you obtained for us yesterday of meriting your approbation, is the regret we feel that it should deprive us, we trust for a short time, of your continued protection. Although so much above any consequence our compliments and congratulations would give you, yet with our own condolence permit us to say we feel and justly appreciate the vigilance, activity, and great gallantry with which on all occasions, and on this occasion particularly, you have sought our honour. As a memorial and tribute of our gratitude we request that you do us the honour to accept the sword which, God grant, you enabled to wield at the head of your brigade'.[21]

When the regiment returned to England, the sword mentioned in the letter was presented to Hussey. On one face it bore the inscription – 'Croix d'Orade, 8th April 1814' and on the reverse 'The officers of the 18th Hussars express by this token their regard for, and confidence in, Major-General R. H. Vivian, who was wounded at the head of their regiment'.

The second is an unequivocal statement in the *United Service Magazine*, which was used, on occasions as an arbitration vehicle in disputes about particular actions. The magazine noted that:

> 'A perusal of the correspondence which took place on the subject in 1840 and 1841 will convince most people that Colonel Vivian did conceive and direct the attack, and that only his wound prevented him personally conducting it . . .'[22]

Hussey returned to England in early June 1814 and, on the 4th of that month he was promoted to the rank of Major-General. He became a Knight Commander of the Bath in the January of the following year.

Meantime, following his abdication, Napoleon was banished to the island of Elba. Peace reigned and, in the short run at least, Hussey could look forward to being with his family without needing to unsheathe his sword again.

NOTES AND REFERENCES

1. Claud Vivian (ibid.). *Richard Hussey Vivian – a memoir*. Letter 19.08.13, p.135.
2. Op. cit., Letter 12.09.13, p.138.
3. Op. cit., Letter 22.09.13, p.143.
4. P. J. Haythornthwaite (ibid.). *Wellington's Military Machine*, p.136.
5. Op. cit., *Lord Vivian – a memoir*. Letter 3.11.13, p.155.
6. Op. cit., Letter 26.11.13, p.165.
7. Sir Archibald Alison (ibid.). *History of Europe*, Volume IX, p.874.
8. Napier, quoted in Claud Vivian (op. cit.), p.173.
9. *Royal United Services Journal* 1, October 1896.
10. Claud Vivian (op. cit.), Letter 14 January 1814, p.187.
11. Op. cit., Letter 21 January 1814, p.190.
12. Op. cit., Letter 27 February 1814, p.199.
13. Napier quoted in Claud Vivian (op. cit.), p.201.
14. Life of Napoleon, quoted in Claud Vivian, Vol. VI, p.598.
15. Op. cit., Letter 18 March 1814, p.226.
16. Op. cit., Letter 24 March 1814, p.230.
17. Op. cit., Letter 1 April 1814, p.235.
18. Op. cit., Journal entry 4 April 1814, p.237.
19. Op. cit., Wellington dispatch, quoted in Claud Vivian, pp.242/3.
20. Op. cit., Letter to Hussey reproduced in Claud Vivian, p.243.
21. Op. cit., Letter quoted in Claud Vivian, p.243.
22. *United Services Magazine*, October 1896.

Chapter Eight

Waterloo

DURING THE TWENTY-FOUR hours before the battle started, the allied communication systems were shown to be inadequate. Fortunately, Wellington decided to go ahead to Quatre Bras to ascertain the position at first hand. He arrived there at 10 a.m. on 16 June and found that a small body of Belgian troops, some Prussian Hussars and infantry constituted the allied army at that site. Wellington approved of the position which the Prussians had taken, for they had effectively used the the folds in the ground to hide their troops. Adjacent to their position was a small river called the Ligny, which had steep banks which were covered with shrubbery. It was about fifteen feet wide and four foot deep, which made it a useful defensive feature. Along its banks were several large farms and a ruined chateau. The Prussians had enhanced these features in several ways. Among other things they had prepared loop-holes in a number of walls and reinforced other buildings to help repel any French attack. At 1 p.m. the Duke met with the Prussian commanders, Blücher and Gneisenau and, with them, watched the French troops, in almost parade-ground mode, assembling in readiness to attack. The defenders did not have to wait too long; Ney's men launched an offensive an hour later.

In typical Napoleonic fashion, Ney began his attack with a heavy cannonade followed by cavalry and infantry involvement. However, as a result of the Prussians' careful preparation, considerable skill, and outstanding courage, they repelled Ney's force. Several factors influenced the outcome of this bombardment and action. Among them were the bravery of the Prussians, the effective pre-planning undertaken by their commanders, and torrential rain which reduced the ground to the consistency of a pudding. However, despite the condition of the ground, the defenders could not understand the inexplicable caution which Ney had shown in not following-up on the ferocious efforts of his infantry, cavalry and guns. By the time the Marshal was ready to attack again, the rain was even heavier. In addition, Wellington's troops were arriving in numbers to re-inforce those of Blücher, and the ground was becoming more and more bog-like as the heavy rain fell on already saturated soil. All in all, the conditions were hardly conducive to the movement of cavalry, guns or soldiers.

The weather was also one of the causes of the late arrival of allied troops at

Quatre Bras, as was poor communication. For example, the delivery of express messages was one activity which left a great deal to be desired, but, it was the torrential rain which caused most problems, for it poured down on roads which were already like bogs. Furthermore, given the volume of traffic which was using them, progress was slow, and it took longer for the allied commanders to reach their objective. Hussey and his men, who were typical of the brigades attempting to reach Quatre Bras, had to travel over forty miles, and, with the roads in poor condition, this lengthened the time taken to cover the distance As a consequence, they were still marching towards the fighting when they ought to have been available to participate, if called upon. These problems were exacerbated by some officers attempting to by-pass poor roads (which were often clogged with troops and guns) by utilising smaller side-roads. One outcome of this was the tendency of some of the columns which were making their way to the scene of the battle to become disoriented and, in effect, lost.

Fortunately, Hussey avoided that difficulty and, when his brigade arrived at Quatre Bras, he and his men took up the position allocated to them on the left of the line. In Uxbridge's scheme of things, Hussey and his brigade were designated 'reserve troops'. Immediately to his right were Vandeleur's cavalry, whilst Picton's Hanoverian Brigades were located to the centre in front of them. The initial tasks of these cavalry men, included skirmishing, scouting for information on enemy movements and supporting/screening the infantry and artillery when they needed to withdraw to one of the positions which Wellington had nominated in his plan. Hussey, meanwhile, had adjusted his own position following a threat from his left. His action in responding to that thrust deterred the French and they withdrew.

These points, then, are indicative of the somewhat inauspicious start to what was to become one of the most famous battles of history – 'Waterloo'. This battle began in earnest at Ligny and near a village called Quatre Bras. Prior to the action, Blücher, the Prussian general and Wellington had discussed the likely pattern of Napoleon's tactical approach. Both men had faced Bonaparte before and believed that he would not change his familiar methods. Typically, Napoleon would start his attack with a major barrage, following which his troops would advance with a view to driving a wedge between two parts of the enemy's force, and destroying the weaker part before turning his attention to the stronger. With Wellington's men arriving after the action had started, the French were not aware of the strength of the army which awaited them.

Consequently, the defenders had an advantage which they sought to exploit. It was important that the two 'wings' of the allied army should be as 'seamless' as possible, and there would not be a weaker/stronger structure of which Bonaparte might take advantage. Wellington's preparation and plan involved his armies fighting from sound defensive positions, and so he was impressed with the quality of the work which his Prussian colleagues had undertaken. Blücher and the Duke were, it appeared, like-minded when considering the advantages of the topography. It was as a result of the meticulous approach to this work of the two generals, that the names of small villages or even farmhouses in the area of battle are burned into the very fabric of military history. Quatre Bras, as will be seen from the map on page 64, stands at the junction of the Charleroi and Brussels roads, was assaulted by Ney, while Ligny, where Napoleon made his earliest attack, is not far away. These places, and a number of others, proved to be hard fought-for locations, and significant numbers of men from the French and allied armies gave their lives in attacking and defending them. As will be seen, each location proved to be an important element in a tactical sense during the broader battle that ensued, which is one reason why they changed hands on several occasions. Initially, it was Blücher and his men alone who bore the brunt of the French onslaught, for it was mid-day before Wellington's forces began to arrive. These re-inforcements were warmly welcomed, in that they provided allied generals with greater resources, but just as importantly, their arrival gave the previously beleaguered Prussian soldiers, a huge psychological boost. In addition it enabled the allies to counter-attack when opportune. So successful were these actions, that the allies won back much of the ground which had been lost, and this despite the fact that the fighting had taken place in dreadful conditions. Once again, torrential rain had turned the field into a veritable quagmire in which men, guns and horses were difficult to move.

Whilst these actions were being fought, the remainder of Wellington's army was arriving at the battle zone, although, at 10 p.m. there were still more units to come. Those which had arrived were absorbed into the battle organisation which Wellington had planned. However, with such large numbers of men, artillery and cavalry *en route,* the roads were more morass-like than ever. In these circumstances, it was inevitable that some of those who were still in transit had lost their bearings. In most cases this problem arose because the officer concerned had attempted to find alternative routes since the main roads were in such poor condition.

Among those who had been separated from their colleagues was Captain Mercer,[1] of the Horse Artillery, who had attached himself to the 23rd Dragoons, only to find that they were unsure as to where they were going. Realising that it seemed to be the case of 'the blind leading the blind', Mercer tried to find a staff officer who was better informed. In his search he came across a senior officer, General Sir Ormsby Vandeleur, but, when the captain approached the general to ask for advice, he was given short shrift. Having been rebuffed, Mercer found a colleague who had been following General Sir Hussey Vivian's cavalry force, and had attached himself to the Cornishman's brigade which, in due course, found its way to the battle zone. There, with little rest, the combined force was soon involved in bloody actions, during which many soldiers on both sides were being maimed or killed. Notwithstanding the conditions, Ligny, in particular was a killing ground, where ferocious hand-to-hand fighting seemed to be never-ending. Despite every effort,

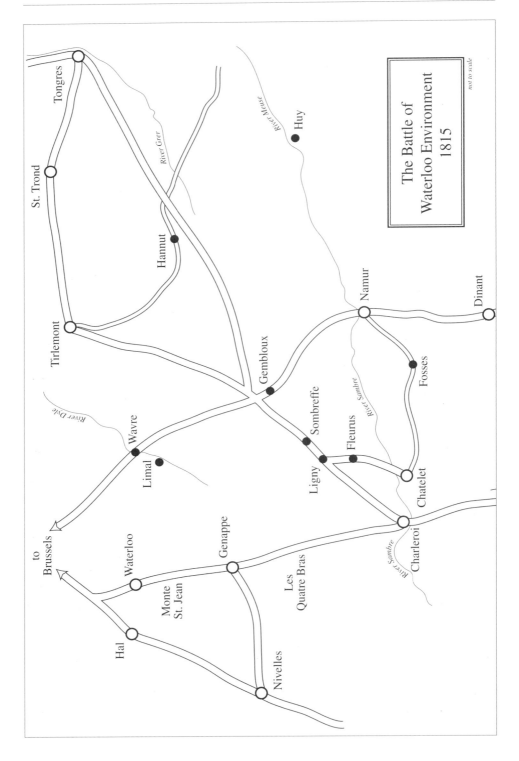

The Battle of
Waterloo Environment
1815

not to scale

towards the evening it looked as if the day was going to end as something of an impasse. There was, however, the advantage from the allied viewpoint, that the arrival of additional men and materials brought them closer to parity with the French.

At Quatre Bras, the rearguard were perplexed by Ney's inactivity, no one could understand why the French marshal had not followed up on his earlier actions. By then, Hussey Vivian's hussars, along with Vandeleur's, were designated 'Reserve Cavalry'. They, and the horse-soldiers in front of them, waited patiently for the French to return to the attack, though for Wellington and Blücher the respite was extremely welcome, for it allowed the infantry to withdraw unscathed through a 'curtain' provided by the cavalry. Once he had seen that all the infantry had retired to their new positions, Wellington demonstrated his antipathy to his mounted colleagues when, as the final soldier passed through, he turned to Uxbridge and said, 'Well, there is the last of the infantry gone, and I don't care now'.[2] Wellington would have cause to change his opinion before many days had passed. In the meantime, after successfully completing their initial task, it was the turn of the cavalry to withdraw as ordered by Uxbridge.

In giving his orders to his senior colleagues, the Duke had emphasised the importance of not becoming involved in fighting until installed in the new locations. The withdrawal had commenced, with Hussey Vivian and Vandeleur posted on the left. During the process, Vivian noted a movement by the French to outflank him. In order to obviate this threat, Hussey, gave his skirmishers the task of containing the French and, as a result, there were testing engagements by units from the Namur road to the eastern fringe of the Bossu wood. Having assisted in delaying the French advance, Hussey and Vandeleur's cavalry went about along a road that led to Thuy. Observing this movement, the French artillery opened up in order to assist the progress of their Lancers and Cuirassiers. Hussey, having given himself breathing space, brought his men to a halt and engaged his guns as the prelude to his men counter-attacking. He was considering giving the order to advance, when a violent thunderstorm broke over the combatants, drenching them and effectively making the aggressive movement of cavalry virtually impossible. Thus it was that, at one fell swoop, the British withdrawal was facilitated, whilst the fervour of the French attackers was somewhat diluted by the soaking they had received.

A feature of the escape route chosen was the river Dyle, and being the senior officer, Vandeleur, had left the task of being last across the bridge situated on the river near Genappe to Hussey Vivian's men. However, he had not completed his withdrawal when the rearguard arrived. Seeing the dangers in the situation Hussey brought up the 10th to support the 1st KGL,* and once Vandeleur's men had all crossed the bridge, the Cornishman pushed the 10th to safety with orders to dismount and provide cover from the other bank, until the British troops were safe. The presence of the bridge which allowed this withdrawal to take place was itself

---

* 'King's German Legion'.

the result of a piece of sound pre-planning. This time Hussey had sent a young artillery officer, Lieutenant Swabey, to reconnoitre the path of the withdrawal and he had located the bridge which, in the event, proved to be so important in enabling the repositioning of the allied cavalry.

Initially, sunrise on 17 June suggested more favourable conditions, and the general opinion was that a better day would herald further fierce action. In the event, dark clouds returned and, by two in the afternoon, they obscured the sun. Not that this stopped the French from attacking. The allies were expecting the French to mount another action during the afternoon, but the enemy started earlier than had been supposed. Prior to that, Captain Mercer, the man who had attached himself to Hussey's brigade *en route* to Quatre Bras, witnessed, from a prime position above the battle area, the coming of the Napoleon's forces. He records that the French came down onto the field 'in three or four dark masses, while their advanced cavalry picket was already driving back our hussars'. The thick black clouds which hung over the heads of the advancing hordes of enemy troops, and which obscured the sun, enhanced rather than diminished the trepidation which the less experienced troops, at least, felt as they waited. Some might have wished that they were elsewhere, but, again Wellington's decision to intermix experienced and inexperienced soldiers, in order that the latter could be 'coached' through an action by the former, was advantageous to the allies.

Mercer, who was without direct orders, on observing the pace of the French advance, decided to reposition his battery slightly. He moved across a fold in the ground which had separated his party from the cavalry of General Vandeleur, and sited his guns afresh. He had completed this manoeuvre when the general stormed up to him in high dudgeon and ordered him to take the guns away. Mercer records that, before he could respond, Lord Uxbridge was on hand to ask him if he was loaded? When the captain said that he was, Uxbridge instructed him to 'give them a round as they rise up the hill, and retire as quickly as possible'. The fighting that day was frenetic and, by the evening many more soldiers on both sides had been killed or wounded. Napoleon appeared to be particularly profligate with his men and resources, which, with the benefit of hindsight, may be interpreted as one indication of his desperate need for victory.[3] This determination to win, no matter how many men and horses were sacrificed, coupled with the matching bravery of the defenders, resulted in the field resembling the yard of a charnel house.

Before going to bed that night of 17 June, Lord Uxbridge asked Hussey Vivian to give him some advice. 'Tomorrow', he said, 'we are going to fight a major battle', and went on to outline his problem which was that, as second in command, he believed that he should be *au fait* with Wellington's plans for the coming action. One of his concerns was the fact that his chief was less than careful about exposing himself to the risk of being killed, which increased the probability of Uxbridge having to take command at some point in the conflict. In preparing for such an eventuality, Uxbridge had attempted to raise the matter with Wellington on a number of occasions, but without success. Given the importance of the coming battle, Uxbridge, wishing to be prepared, wanted advice as to what he should do. Hussey suggested that he might use the Spanish general, Count Alva, as a go-between, but in the end, Wellington and Uxbridge discussed the issue themselves. The outcome, however, was less than helpful for the second-in-command. The Duke asked Uxbridge, who would be the first to attack on the morrow? The answer was clear – Napoleon. Wellington then pointed out that he had not been given any indication by his enemy as to what the French were going to do. Consequently, he was not in a position to help Uxbridge. This ended the discussion, though, before Uxbridge left, Wellington wished him good night, adding 'There is one thing certain, Uxbridge, that is that, whatever happens, you and I will do our duty' and, after shaking hands, the men went to their beds, for it was to be a short night of rest.[4]

Between 10 and 11 o'clock the following morning the allied cavalry moved into the positions to which they had been allocated. Wellington, in line with his tactical approach, selected Mont-Saint-Jean as the area in which he was going to fight. His planning relied on the timely arrival of Blücher's cavalry. Just as the Duke had come to the aid of Blücher, so the Prussian had promised to reciprocate, with his cavalry scheduled to arrive by mid-day on 18 June. In the event, the cavalry, his was a key element of the re-inforcements, did not arrive until 4.30 p.m. Nevertheless, whilst they were late in arriving, as had happened when the boot had been on the other foot, the newcomers provided the existing soldiers not only with extra resources, but also boosted morale in the allied camp. Furthermore, observing the arrival of fresh men, guns and horses coming to join Wellington and Blücher, when they were tired from fighting for their lives during most of the previous day, the French soldiery must have been rather concerned.

Meanwhile, Napoleon, assuming that Blücher, following his defeat at Ligny, would be a softer target in the next phase of the battle, believed that the Prussians, if faced with another massive attack, would be likely to give way. Hussey Vivian's initial part in the coming battle was to take position, as reserve cavalry, on the left of Wellington's line. From that sector of the battlefield, he was to send out scouts/skirmishers, not only to obtain intelligence on the movements of French troops, but also to ascertain the time of arrival of Blücher's cavalry. By then, Hussey's brigade had been among the least used forces in the battle. It was not surprising, therefore, that the cavalry men under his command should be seeking the opportunity to get involved in the fighting. That is what they had trained to do. Surely, they must have thought, this is our chance to do our duty and gain something of the glory for our regiment from the battle now in progress.

In typical fashion, Napoleon's next onslaught began with a heavy barrage. The present Marquess of Anglesey described the scene:

'The two armies faced each other from opposing ridges across a gently sloping valley, the distance being nowhere much more than a thousand yards. Each army presented a front of about three miles . . . Wellington chose his ground with his usual skills'.[5]

The Duke had, indeed, selected his ground with great care. Certainly, the typography was in his favour. When the French began their approach, their intentions could be gauged from the allied position with reasonable accuracy. Conversely, many of the allied force were hidden from the enemy's view in folds in the ground. Thus, Wellington had the advantage of seeing what the deployment of French troops, suggested about their intentions. Napoleon, on the other hand, could only estimate where and in what strength the allied forces were positioned?

As noon approached, Napoleon launched an attack on Wellington's flank near Chateau de Hougoumont. It was to have been a diversionary action, but the initial thinking of Napoleon and his staff was forgotten as the battle flowed. Starting with an unprecedented barrage from a heavily reinforced battery. Napoleon believed that, not only would this severely damage the allied defences, but the casualties which would arise, would force the Duke to draw more troops to that sector, thus weakening his right centre, which was Bonaparte's favoured target. Not only could the positioning of the dozens of extra French guns on the opposite ridge be seen from that occupied by the allies, so could the manoeuvring of the French troops. Presumably, Napoleon deliberately made much of this parading in order to cause consternation among his opponents, for it was an awesome sight, as seven battalions of infantry, preceded by lancers, advanced towards the allied line. Initially, the gallant defence of allied troops hidden in the wood adjacent to the chateau, resulted in decimation of the oncoming French. However, with a shortage of ammunition hampering them as they fought to stem the enemy's advance, and facing a seemingly endless progression of Napoleon's soldiers, the allied sharpshooters were forced to withdraw. This they did in good order, falling back into the chateau, which they continued to defend with great courage. Indeed, it was estimated that 1,500 enemy troops had been killed in clearing the wood. Many more were to perish as the French became obsessed with capturing the building.

Another cannonade began at midday and continued without respite for ninety minutes. When the barrage opened up, the Union Brigade of cavalry was unfortunate enough to find itself in the precise position which the French had estimated allied troops would be gathered. In order to reduce the chances of being caught in this way, the brigade moved to its left. However, by this time, the indications were that the French were intent on attacking elsewhere. When the barrage was lifted, the soldiers who awaited the attack, many of them young and inexperienced, must have been affected by the sight and sound of the hordes of oncoming enemy. Fortunately, Wellington had ensured that there were always experienced soldiers to support and encourage the newcomers as they awaited the coming of the French. It is interesting to speculate whether the experienced men would have been exhorting their younger colleagues (à la a Hollywood epic relating to this period) to hold fast until they could see the whites of the eyes of the oncoming French. Nonetheless, the innermost concerns of the veterans as well as those who had little experience of battle, must have been affected by the cacophony of noise which emerged from the massed ranks of the advancing French army. Indeed, it would have been surprising if the waiting allied troops were not affected in that way. The martial sounds created by hundreds of drums which beat the *pas de charge*, and by the thousands of French voices which roared out time and again, '*Vive l'Empereur*', when taken together, it must have been a production to strike terror into opponents hearts. Cecil B. de Milne would, surely, have approved.

Uxbridge had given strict instructions to the allied artillery men not to waste ammunition by firing back at the French batteries. Rather they were ordered to fire shot, shell and canister, as quickly and effectively as possible into the advancing French ranks, and as many rounds as they could, before withdrawing into the nearest square. One result of this firing was carnage of a terrifying extent, yet the French still continued to advance, and there were several occasions when it looked as if Napoleon's masses were winning the battle. As the tide of battle ebbed and flowed, the situation was analogous to a bare-knuckle fight, in which one boxer would be sent crashing to the canvas, only to rise again and turn the tables on his opponent with a ferocious attack of his own. In general, however, the various actions fought on 17 June had been shaded in favour of the French. In boxing parlance, they were 'ahead on points'. Yet the contest was still on-going, and the allies, on that Sunday, 18 June 1815, had to fight at their best to gain the upper hand.

After repelling a French attack, Uxbridge decided to counter-attack with his heavy brigades. At first the action looked to be brilliantly successful, and in the early stages two 'Eagles'[6] and 3,000 prisoners were captured, but, then, things started to go wrong. Initially, the Greys advanced, while the Royals and the Inniskillings were to join them in line. Coming up the slope to the crest of the ridge above them, the cavalry men, using natural cover effectively, exploded onto the downward slope. Surprise was on their side, and despite the efficiency of the French infantry in using musket fire, they were unable to form squares in time to receive the British cavalry. Considerable progress was made as, on the left, the Inniskillings savaged a column of French troops, whilst those on the right, with sabre and hoof, were creating havoc in another brigade. Unfortunately, the Greys, in their enthusiasm for the chase, charged on, only to find that the French who made up the next section of their advancing army, had formed an effective square which took advantage of what, by then, were blown horses and weary arms. Almost at point blank range the French took their toll on the Heavy Brigades.

Nor was that the end of the matter. The Royals, who had been frustrated by hedges, which forced them to make a significant detour, arrived too late to support the Greys, but they burst onto the field and, seeing the French square still in being, charged at an angle, and with frightening effect, slashed, chopped and stabbed Napoleon's troops. Lord Uxbridge, himself, at the head of the 2nd Life Guards which were followed closely by the remaining elements of the Union Brigade, added sabre power and drove the enemy back in some disorder. Many lives were lost in the process and, for Uxbridge, the loss of so many men was something with which troubled him for the rest of his life. Despite these issues, the attacks did contribute to the overall victory, if only because no one could recall a more audacious and glorious action in the history of British cavalry. Uxbridge, subsequently re-counted the problem he faced in trying to rally his colleagues, and reported that they could not, or did not want to hear his Lordship's verbal instructions or sign language.

As well as those captured, thousands of Frenchmen fled, but, in the midst of the euphoria which the early action had aroused, there remained concern in the allied camp. When Napoleon's artillery resumed its barrage to some effect, and as shot and shell inflicted their carnage on British lines, those who were observing the build-up of the next French attack were under no illusion; an onslaught was imminent. Nonetheless, they were puzzled by the latest intelligence which had been received, for it suggested that Bonaparte was to field forty squadrons of cavalry when he attacked. This information caused many an eyebrow to be raised, for received wisdom suggested that such an assault against a prepared defensive line would not be successful and would result in huge losses for the attacking army. Yet, following the French cannonade, Napoleon's men began their advance, drums beating, and voices roaring out their battle cry, 'Vive l'Empereur'. Whilst most of the allied troops who waited that day had experienced at least one such an attack, psychologically, the total production remained a threatening precursor to the fighting which was to come.

In all, it was an expensive action from the point of view of both parties, but it was not to end there. A squadron of the Royals, fresh to the field, used the topo-graphy to give them the advantage of surprise, and set upon the remaining French with lethal purpose. Seeing that charge, Napoleon himself, gave the order for his cuirassiers to give the allied cavalrymen a taste of their own medicine. From their relatively elevated position, the remaining allied cavalry brigades were able to watch the ebb and flow of the action. After the Netherlands Light Brigade had galloped to the assistance of the remaining allied forces, Hussey Vivian's troops and those of Vandeleur were accused by General Muffling (the Prussian Military Attaché) of 'maintaining masterly inactivity'[7] when comrades were in need of assistance. Both men claimed that they were obeying the orders of the Duke, which precluded them from getting involved in any conflict unless he or Uxbridge gave such instruction. Presumably, the general was not satisfied with their answer, for he sought verification from the Duke, himself. Wellington's reply was unequivocal: 'The two generals were perfectly correct in their answer, for had they made such an onslaught without my permission, even though the greatest success had crowned their attempt, I must have brought them to a court-martial'.

As the day wore on, the French attacked with great ferocity on at least three occasions. Ney's attempts to break through, however, were repulsed by the allied defenders, but many lives were lost on both sides. In addition, fatigue was beginning to play a part, with all concerned wishing for some respite. For their part, the French continued to give the impression that they were unconcerned as to how many of their men, horses and guns were lost, for they remained aggressive despite the carnage which allied guns, men and horses had inflicted. The defenders must have wondered if Napoleon had an unending supply of troops and equipment. Meantime, once Uxbridge had ensured that the Prussian cavalry had arrived, he posted them to the positions previously manned by Hussey Vivian and Vandeleur, and moved these brigades into the centre of the allied line. According to Uxbridge, 'Vivian, with his usual alertness, had forestalled the instruction, and the exchange took place smoothly'.[8]

While matters seemed evenly balanced, there was a growing feeling that the advantage seemed to be swinging back to the Allies, and their officers were contemplating the timing of attacks of their own, Hussey among them, though he had expected Lord Uxbridge to join him in the initial attack. Unfortunately, the best-laid plans of mice and men go astray, and so they did on this occasion. The story behind his Lordship's failure to appear has found its way into the very fabric of British military history and provided Uxbridge, who had taken an active rôle in many of the campaigns, with a new nickname – 'One leg'. It was recorded that, just as Hussey Vivian gave the order to advance, Lord Uxbridge was struck by a grapeshot on his right knee. The joint was shattered by the blow. The story goes that, at the time of the incident, Uxbridge was about to take leave of Wellington, in order to join Hussey Vivian, when, almost casually, he exclaimed, 'By God, sir, I've lost my leg!' Wellington, removing his telescope from his eye, viewed the mangled limb, and replied, 'By God, sir, so you have'; after which he renewed his scrutiny of the field of battle.[9]

During the afternoon of 18 June, around the time when ladies and gentlemen in England drank their tea, Napoleon was beginning to harbour doubts about the outcome of the battle with Wellington. In order to promote his political and military objectives he needed to win a swift victory when, having defeated the English duke, it would enable him to march on Brussels. Uncertain though Napoleon might have been, being something of a gambler, he decided to mount another major attack on the allied lines. It was to prove to be his last throw of the dice.

As a prelude to the French onslaught, Napoleon's guns pounded the allied lines with the heaviest, concentrated artillery barrage which anyone of the united force had ever experienced. In turn, Wellington, after ordering squares to be formed to repel the French cavalry, issued instructions to his gunners. He urged them to fire as many rounds as possible into the on-coming cuirassiers and lancers, before withdrawing to the nearest square. Thus it was that, when the French began to advance, the gunners had double-loaded with canister and shot, and bided their time until the enemy cavalry was within a prescribed distance. Whilst the initial line of French horsemen were decimated by the deadliness of the allied fire, their survivors, charged on, with considerable bravery, taking advantage of the reach of their lances, and many allied soldiers were wounded or killed in the process. Nonetheless, having lost so many men, the French had little alternative but to withdraw what remained of their force, and attempt to reorganise. Despite the unyielding resolve of the allied troops, Napoleon continued to attack in numbers and both sides suffered heavy casualties. By the evening, developments on the field had confirmed what Wellington and his staff had concluded earlier in the day. The French were gambling on breaking through, no matter what the cost in men, horses and equipment might be. With little sign that the threat from the French was abating, Wellington decided to use his reserves, and moved Hussey Vivian's brigade and that of Vandeleur to the centre. This was the *raison d'être* of the duke's back-up cavalry. They could be brought to the battle field, in order to provide a zest and freshness which would give them and his army advantage over battle-weary opponents.

Yet, the benefits stemming from the fresh resource would not be seen immediately. Napoleon, in the belief that, earlier, his troops had gained the upper hand at Quatre Bras and Ligny, convinced himself that, one more major attack could finish the task in his favour. He had boasted, before the battle began, that the odds on him winning were loaded in his favour. He was not as certain in his own mind as preparations for the attack were completed, but, somehow, he drew deeply on his well of self-confidence, and pushed the doubts out of his mind. Those soldiers who had listened to Napoleon's pre-battle talk, responded to his urgings; the Emperor would lead them and he would 'sup in Brussels'. There followed several major attacks on the allied lines, each of which was repelled by Wellington's forces, though at considerable cost to both sides.

During this period, Hussey Vivian was involved in the process of providing protection to enable retiring allied troops to filter through the cavalry lines to their new positions. In his journal he described the situation in which he found himself, and there is no doubt that he took very seriously the responsibility for assisting his comrades as they sought the haven of their own lines. Having stayed in line with his brigade, whilst the foot soldiers and the survivors of the Heavy Brigade made their way to the rear, he wrote in his journal, 'I then remained for about a half hour, exposed to shot, shell and musketry. How a man can escape is to me a miracle'.

Since Hussey went into battle on a milk-white horse, which made him an obvious target, it would appear that he was not indulging in hyperbole. It is also clear that he did his duty, despite whatever fear he might have felt in being exposed. True heroes have to overcome fear in whatever way they can devise.[10]

There followed a period in which Napoleon threw everything into what turned out to be a last desperate action. Before mounting the attack he addressed his 'children' in his usual pre-battle style, saying that he wanted to take supper in Brussels and it was up to them to make a pathway for him. Such was Napoleon's Swami-like relationship with his troops, that they went to war motivated to a level of fervour that must have seemed unquenchable to the waiting allies. But Wellington and his senior colleagues were also well-versed in motivating troops, and Hussey Vivian was amongst those who roused the spirits of the soldiers under his command. With clouds of gun smoke hanging over the field of battle, the Brunswickers and the Nassauers, together with the British, surged forward in counter-attack. As the combatants approached each other, the cacophony of sounds of the firing of guns, muskets, and rifles, and the cheering and counter cheering of the soldiers, contributed to the creation of a fitting atmosphere for what would prove to be a decisive action. Many of those who survived the battle were said to have been affected by that experience for the remainder of their lives. Furthermore, when the sounds mentioned above were superimposed upon those of the clash of sabre with sabre, with lance, and with bayonet, the grunts and groans, the screams for help of soldiers from both armies, the pitiful sounds coming from injured horses and the associated battle cries which filled the air, it was a cruel environment. As he waited, and witnessed the bedraggled allied soldiers making their way through his cavalry to their new positions, Hussey was particularly moved by Lord Edward Somerset's response to the question, 'Where are your Brigades?' Somerset and his colleagues, the Heavies, had left their lines with 2,000 cavalrymen. In response he said, with great sadness in his voice, 'Just us', and pointed to the ground. There were less than 200 left of a proud force of dragoons.[11]

Hussey's command at the battle of Waterloo, comprised the 10th Prince of Wales Hussars, the 18th Hussars, and the 1st Hussars of the Kings German Legion. Along with Vandeleur's brigade, Hussey and his men were located on the left. At around eleven o'clock the French began an attack on a wood from which the footguards were causing them considerable trouble. In expectation of this action, the whole line moved up into position. In his diary, Hussey noted that they saw the French, in 'enormous masses' manoeuvring on the side of the hill opposite them. Everything pointed to a major attack, typical of Napoleon. The now familiar pattern of a heavy cannonade, followed by action involving cavalry whose aim was to was to weaken the position of the defenders in readiness for infantry involvement. In that instance the high road, which was near the centre of the Allied line, appeared to be the target. Wave after wave French troops pounded the allied positions, but the defenders did not give way, as the squares which they set up stood firm, while their guns raked the oncoming French with deadly fire. Meanwhile, the allied cavalry was taking the initiative on several fronts. Hussey's men, to their relief, were among those who took battle to the French.

Because of the extent of the gun-smoke hanging over the field of battle, neither side could see, clearly enough, what the other was intending to do. In Hussey's case, thanks to a sudden gust of wind, momentarily, the fog-like cover was dispersed in one sector. To Hussey's surprise, he found that the French were withdrawing rather than massing for another attack. Elsewhere, the Prussians were still locked in battle, with the enemy. But Hussey saw this as 'the moment to attack and move forward' and led the 10th in challenging a body of cuirassiers and lancers on the French left. Following what was a successful action there, he moved to lead the 18th (who had been standing in reserve) in attacking another body of French horsemen who were assisting in the protection of a square made up of the famous Imperial Guard. Hussey's men not only defeated the French, but they also captured fourteen pieces of cannon.

In the next hour, Lord Greenock brought Hussey instructions to move to his right so as to enable the movement of the infantry. This he did and then made the 10th the leading arm, with the 18th in the second line and 1st Hussars KGL in the rear. With similar developments elsewhere in the front, Hussey and his men were champing at the bit, and there was genuine disappointment when Sir Colin Campbell gave Hussey an order from Wellington to the effect that he was not to attack before the infantry came up. Hussey, believing that his brigade would lose momentum if they did not follow-through, argued that there were French cavalry blocking the path of the footsoldiers, and that it would be necessary to defeat them before pushing the infantry forward. In minutes Hussey had convinced Greenock of the correctness of his assessment and had ordered the 10th Hussars to form up in readiness for further advance, whilst the other two regiments were to form a supporting line. As soon as the first squadron was in place, Hussey ordered and headed the charge, following which the 2nd Light Dragoons came up on the right. After some confusion caused by a body of Cuirassiers, progress continued to be made. No sooner had the 10th made aggressive contact with the enemy, than the French on their left were in full flight. At that point, Hussey Vivian, having learnt the lesson about over-zealous chase, called a halt and returned as quickly as possible, so that he might lead the 18th Hussars in the next attack.

Wellington, who had observed the effective action of Hussey and his troops against the enemy's forces in the area near La Belle Alliance, the very heart of Napoleon's position, plus the triumphant march of the infantry under Buklow, ordered the general advance. As he did so, he might well have been examining his reticence to fully embrace the potential of well-led cavalry.

As will be seen from the earlier material in this book, Hussey, despite his private concerns about staying alive during a battle, always faced up to 'doing his duty'. An incident during the action described earlier, is indicative of the good fortune which he always recognised had been his during his military career.

In transferring from the 10th to lead the 18th, he was assailed by a lone cuirassier. By then Hussey had his right arm in a sling, which meant that he could only use it to hold the reins of his horse. He wrote in his journal:

> 'I was fortunate enough to give him (the Frenchman) a thrust in the neck with my left hand . . . and, at that moment I was joined by my little German orderly, who cut the fellow off his horse'.[12]

On arrival at the 18th, Hussey urged the troops on: 'Come on my lads, you will, I know follow me'. Presumably speaking for his comrades, Sergeant-Major Jeffs responded: 'Yes, General! To Hell if you will lead us'.[13]

Thus it was that the 18th attacked the second body of French cavalry which was acting as a shield in support of the square comprised, largely of the Imperial Guard. Such was the success of the action that, whilst the square was not broken, as such, it was impotent enough to allow the British to capture fourteen pieces of cannon. In his journal entry, two days later, Hussey paid tribute to his brigades by arguing that, 'The enemy was routed by the intrepidity and gallantry of this regiment, and the Artillery men cut down at their guns'.[14]

Wellington was the victor and, no doubt, Uxbridge would find the opportunity to remind the Duke of the important part played by the cavalry in gaining the victory over Napoleon. As the following example illustrates, Hussey Vivian was not backward in allotting praise to other parties. Given the scale and importance of the battle to the whole of Europe, it was not surprising that each of the countries which made up the alliance, wanted to receive a share of the glory. This had the effect of encouraging nationalistic xenophobia, particularly in Great Britain, where some well-connected parties were attempting to minimise the part played by the Prussians in gaining the victory. Hussey, in responding to a myopic argument from one such person replied:

> 'Those are most unjust to the Prussians who refuse them their full share of the credit'.[15]

This typical Richard Hussey-Vivian response speaks volumes for his inherent 'fairness'. He had come a long way in many senses since he first joined the army, but his fundamental predilections, which bore the hallmark of a sound Cornish upbringing, remained in him unchanged.

NOTES AND REFERENCES

1. D. Hamilton-Williams (ibid.). *Waterloo – New Perspectives*, (1993), p.201.
2. Marquess of Anglesey (ibid.). *One Leg* (1971), p.128.
3. D. Hamilton-Williams (op. cit.), pp.251/2.
4. Marquess of Anglesey (op. cit.), pp.132-3.
5. Marquess of Anglesey (op. cit.), p.134.
6. When Napoleon returned to France from exile, he was marching north when he made contact with the 5th and the 7th Regiments of foot. The colonel in charge of the 7th (Bodoyere) came forward to greet Bonaparte, who commented on the 'standards' which the colonel's regiment was carrying. These were the famous 'eagles', which the Republican had introduced into his army's structure, and were totems which were both a rallying symbol and a focal point to which the soldiers of a particular army unit might relate. For many, the 'eagle' help generate pride in the group to which each soldier belonged. The standards had to be hidden when the French royal house had been restored. They were banned on the grounds that they were a symbol of Napoleon's reign, and because the 'eagle' was superimposed over the country's flag.

   The following day, Napoleon wasted no time in arranging for a proclamation to be posted in every town, city of village of France. Again, the image of the 'eagle' was used as a rallying image. Napoleon started with:

   > 'We were NOT defeated' and, after urging Frenchmen to re-join their emperor, used the eagle to stir the imaginations of those who read the poster. He added: 'Victory will advance at a charge; the eagle, with the national colours, will fly from steeple to steeple all the way to the towers of Notre Dame . . .'

   Because of its importance both to the individual unit and the army as a whole, the eagle was revered by the troops of Napoleon and whoever carried the standard would guard it with his life. Consequently, to seize an eagle from the French was a highly regarded feat in the eyes of the allied forces.

7. Claud Vivian (ibid.). *Richard Hussey Vivian – a memoir* (1897) p.302.
8. Marquess of Anglesey (op. cit.), pp.146/7.
9. Philip J. Haythornthwaite (ibid.). *Wellington's Military Machine* (1989) p.145.
10. Claud Vivian (op. cit), p.303.
11. Claud Vivian (op. cit.), p.306.
12. Claud Vivian (op. cit.), p.309.
13. W. H. Tregelles (ibid.). *Some Cornish Worthies*, p.356.
14. Claud Vivian (op. cit.), p.310.
15. Philip J. Haythornthwaite (op. cit.), p.145.

Chapter Nine

An Alternative Viewpoint

THERE IS A CYNICAL view of History which suggests that, at least some of those who write about it, often use ink made from liquid prejudice. A less subtle criticism is said to have been voiced by Henry Ford, the US motor-car baron; his notorious view of the subject being, 'All History is bunk'. On the other hand, in the opinion of leading historians, intelligent reading of the subject can be beneficial. Joseph Roux,[1] a French philosopher, supports that view and suggests one such benefit. He argues that it provides the principal means of 'becoming a contemporary of all ages and a fellow citizen of all people'. In addition, the pragmatist would argue that man can learn from history and, to quote a well-known maxim, that 'there's nothing new under the sun'.

In all probability, the reader will be able to identify with some aspect of both sides of the argument. For example, those who have read biographies of leading political figures (and, in particular, autobiographies), or read reviews of this type of publication, will be aware of the tendency of some authors to re-arrange history. On the other hand, a great deal of corporate legislation in this and other countries, is in being because of what happened in the past. An obvious example of this being the anti-monopoly legislation.

With respect to the present text, those who teach the skills of warfare would be considerably disadvantaged if they were not able to draw upon historical material. Analysis of such data allows consideration of the environment in which major battles were fought, and the benefits and disadvantages of particular approaches. Because that is so, the army has long-standing experience of collecting reports from the field, in order that, in retrospect, it will be able to learn from its experience and use that learning for training purposes.

This book is concerned with the life, as a soldier, of Richard Hussey Vivian (1775-1841). It is the outcome of a sincere attempt to produce an objective record of the military life of a man who, if he had done nothing else, gained a remarkable number of honours in the course of a lengthy career as a soldier. Of necessity, the author has had to sieve and interpret information gleaned from a variety of sources. In the process, it has been necessary to consider many issues which arose during Hussey's lifetime in the army, and their impact on other personalities with whom he made contact during that period, as well upon himself.

WATERLOO

The caveats which the foregoing discussion suggests, are interesting in themselves, but, in the context of military history, it is also necessary to be aware of others. There is a great deal of literature which relates to the period in which Hussey Vivian served in the British army but, without doubt, the final battle in which he fought – Waterloo – gave rise to more publications than any other. In addition, because of the number of different countries which were involved in the action, that literature was published in more languages than had been the case with any other conflict. Furthermore, over the years, the battle has attracted the attention of many scholars, some of whom have undertaken long and detailed research in order to add to our understanding of the event. A broad objective of these researchers has been to develop as definitive a record of the famous battle as possible, though, given that it was fought almost two centuries ago, the task is very demanding. As the present Marquess of Anglesey put it in the foreword to a leading text on Waterloo:

> 'I'll wager that no one who reads David Hamilton-Williams' new perspectives approach will doubt that the re-assessment he offers is an essential step towards the truth. Definitive, of course, it is not, for how can there ever be a complete picture of any human activity in which large numbers are killed and of which the majority fail to give an account . . . The military historian can only hope to add veracity, and correct lies and inaccuracies'.[2]

Philip Haythornthwaite, another prominent Waterloo authority, adds further caution for consideration here. For example, he offers Wellington's own comment about 'contemporary sources in which the possibility of inaccuracy must be taken into account'. The Duke, writing to Robert Craufurd on 23 July 1810, remarked that:

> 'As soon as an accident happens, every man who can write, and who has a friend who can read, sits down to write his own account of what he does not know, and his comments on what he does not understand'.[3]

Nevertheless, as Haythornthwaite points out, many contemporary accounts can be shown to be extremely accurate, at least when describing events which fell within the reporter's personal experience. In acknowledging that inaccuracies can occur, he argues that some writers have tended to distort facts to fulfil a variety of motives ranging from personal aggrandisement to national bias.

It is evident that, given the need for the army to be able to record the progress of battles, and, accepting the particular issues which relate to the military field, officers will have received some training in undertaking the work. Nevertheless, the individuals involved will still be possessed of different levels of skill in acting in, recalling and summarising the 'story'. Few men are gifted with total recall, or comprehensive observational ability, particularly when the fighting has been hand-to-hand. After all, it must be enough to stay alive, without attempting to think about what will be written when describing the action.

The comments of the Marquess of Anglesey, referred to earlier, put the dilemma into perspective, particularly his telling remark that only survivors report. There is, also, the point that such reports largely reflect the extent of the involvement of the individual, the accidents of time and place, as well as his personal predilections. Of course, the academics who work in the field are aware of these issues and of their potential impact upon the conclusions which they draw from the data, but it is right and proper to remind ourselves of some of the issues which are involved. The problems surrounding one of these relate to the passage of time between the event and the production of the particular report. One example of this was an account sent to Captain Siborne by a Colonel Childers in 1845. Referring to an account of an action during Waterloo and involving Lieut-General Sleigh, Childers rather testily wrote:

> 'It only shows how hopeless it is to expect (after such a lapse of time) an account from those who were actors in what took place, in which all should agree. For my part, I do not even recollect the bridge to which the Lieut.-General refers'.[4]

The Captain Siborne mentioned here was an ensign in the 1st Battalion, 9th Foot. He did not take part in the Battle of Waterloo, but subsequently served in the Army of Occupation in Paris. While he was there, he saw military models in the form of three-dimensional topographical maps on display at Les Invalides. He was taken with the idea of using such maps as aids in planning for military purposes. Like any young enthusiast, he did his best to get his idea accepted by his superiors. In due course, Lord Hill gave official sanction for the project and promised financial assistance. In addition, Siborne was given permission to correspond with British officers who had taken part in the battle. Eventually, the young captain, after receiving many accounts recalling the involvement of the respondents in many sectors of the battle, produced what was regarded as being the 'bible' of the battle. When the record was published, it was deemed to have been based upon the 'irrefutable evidence of officers and gentlemen' so that no one thought to question it. As will be noted from the extract from the letter from Colonel Childers, reproduced above, Siborne's intention was to get agreement from a group of people who were involved in particular events, regarding what actually occurred.

Unfortunately, Siborne had understated the costs which would be incurred in undertaking the task, the funds promised by the authorities proved to be inadequate, and, as a result, he sunk into poverty. Despite attempting to alleviate his financial problems by building a topographical model of the Waterloo battlefield and exhibiting it in order to boost his income, he could not close the gap between his earnings and his expenditure. At one stage, he wrote to many of the officers who had responded to his survey, requesting a loan of £5 or £10. Siborne believed he could repay these loans from income derived from putting the model on show to the public. Sadly, it was not to be!

In his discussion relating to the Siborne affair, David Hamilton-Williams, points out that the captain's commanding officer at the time when the letters soliciting funds from each respondent, were circulated, was Richard Hussey Vivian and, it appears, that Vivian agreed to lend Siborne £1,000. It is evident from the tone of his comments on Siborne's work that, as a professional military historian, David Hamilton-Williams was incensed when it became apparent that the captain's report, which had been the 'bible' of the battle, was flawed. In line with the Marquess of Anglesey's description of the rôle open to the military scholar, quoted earlier, he saw his task as being to 'add veracity and correct lies and inaccuracies'. The justifiable criticism of Siborne which emerged following the exposé showed the extent of Hamilton-Williams's concern for the field of study in which he worked. He wrote:

> 'No one Englishman had so great an influence on the English language Historiography of the Battle of Waterloo as Captain William Siborne. So heavy has been Siborne's hand on the memory of the event that all histories of it to date, including those written by Historians of other nations involved, depend fundamentally on his interpretation'.[5]

In his discussion about the many issues which the exposé uncovered, Hamilton-Williams leaves little to the imagination of the reader, when he writes: 'From now (from the loan of £1,000) the objectivity which had marked Siborne's approach to the project became a luxury which he could no longer afford'. By implication, at least, there is the suggestion here that Hussey Vivian was party to any alterations being made in order to show him in better light than might otherwise have been the case. This, of course, is a serious charge which, having spent the best part of two years 'getting to know' Richard Hussey Vivian while researching his life, the writer finds it difficult to believe.

Whatever his short-comings, Vivian was not stupid. He would have known that when subscriptions were made to some cause, lists of donors would have appeared in the newspapers of the day, with the most generous amount heading the list. Indeed, he made no secret of his support for Siborne. The very transparency of his gesture suggests a different motive. Perhaps his was a genuine attempt to be the patron of a young man with a creative idea who had served under him. In addition, there was the question of the honour of the regiment, which might have been another factor in Vivian's thinking.

There is, too, the evidence of the quality and longevity of Hussey Vivian's relationships with people. Among his many associations was that with William Paget (who became the Earl of Uxbridge, and subsequently the Marquess of Anglesey). The two men were not only colleagues in the army, but firm friends over many years, and when such associations are considered, one of the key factors in their continuing success is mutual trust. Throughout this book, that trust is evident. For example, when Uxbridge, as he was then, was challenged to a duel by the brother of Lady Charlotte Wellesley (Capt. Cadogan), Hussey Vivian stood as his second; when Uxbridge was concerned about Wellington's battle plans, he turned to Hussey for advice; together they saved a yacht in which they had been sailing from capsizing, and, after Uxbridge had lost his leg, he asked Hussey for his opinion regarding the decision he had taken to have the leg amputated.

There are numerous other incidents which are included in the literature which show Hussey Vivian in good light. One such example is the comment by the present Marquess of Anglesey relating to the state of British Cavalry at the time Uxbridge began to exercise an influence on the training and deployment of the horse soldiers. The Marquess wrote: 'In his Brigade commanders he was well-served, Hussey Vivian and Colquhoun Grant were old friends'.[6] Presumably the friendship which both these men enjoyed with the first marquess was also relevant in respect of their performance as soldiers. Sir E. Wood, who wrote the recognised work, *Cavalry at Waterloo*, tells us something about Hussey's keenness to lead his men into battle:

> 'Modern cavalry soldiers who read these articles will be astonished to see how the generals displaced the commanding officers in leading charges.
> Vivian went so far to halt his second line (the 18th) till he could charge with his first line (the 10th) and return to lead the 18th. He only failed to lead the third regiment when the darkness prevented further attacks being executed'.[7]

Finally, following a discussion regarding the order in which Hussey Vivian's men and those of Vandeleur went into battle, Vivian after praising his brigades, and giving the reason for his request for confirmation, said:

> 'Truth is history, and history without truth does not deserve the name; and I am anxious for the sake of the gallant men that I commanded, that one day at least the truth may be known'.[8]

Richard Hussey Vivian was a man who was dedicated to doing his duty. There are numerous examples in this book of his desire to meet the needs evident in a particular situation with his abilities to match them.

This short chapter is included here because the writer believes that Hussey was consistent in his consideration of the action which should be taken in the many situations which he faced as an army officer. Duty was at the front of his mind. Because that is so, to the present writer, it seems highly unlikely that he would deliberately falsify the accurate recording of history.

*   *   *

The list which follows is indicative of what other people thought of Richard Hussey Vivian:

- One of Wellington's dispatches was full of praise following the outstanding performance of the 18th Hussars at Croix d'Orde when, under the immediate command of Colonel Vivian, 'secured an important bridge with a most gallant attack upon a superior body of the enemy . . . Colonel Vivian was unfortunately wounded upon this occasion and I am afraid I shall lose his services for some time.'

- During his time in hospital, Hussey received a warm letter from the officers of 18th Hussars emphasising their support, gratitude and approbation and, when in early June 1814 Hussey Vivian came back to England, on the 4th of the month his colleagues presented him with a sword. On one side of the blade was engraved '8 April 1814 Croix d'Orde' with their message of approbation on the other.

- Hussey was appointed to the Sussex Military District and promoted to Major General on 4th June 1814 and Knight Commander of the Bath in January 1815. Then following Waterloo:

- For his services at Waterloo, Vivian was mentioned in dispatches and received the thanks of both Houses of Parliament.

- After the Battle, Vivian was presented with the order of Maria Theresa (Austria); with the Order of St. Wladimir (Russia).

- In 1818, when drastic reductions in army numbers resulted in the 18th Hussars disbanding, the soldiers of the regiment presented Hussey Vivian with a silver trumpet.

- The University of Oxford accorded to him the high honour of D.C.L.

- In 1827 he was given a colonelcy of the Life Guards.

- In 1830, William IV made him a Grand Cross of the Royal Hanoverian Order of Guelph.

- On 11 August 1841, Hussey became Baron Vivian of Glynn and Truro.

*   *   *

A Colonel Taylor of the 10th Hussars provided Hussey with a poem, written especially for him after Waterloo:

> From the left flank, in column, winding far,
> Speeds with a whirlwind's force the swift hussar;
> Tho' to their thundering hoofs the plain resounds
> Still cautious discipline their ardour bounds,
> Who, with a hero's port and lofty form
> With waving sabre onward guides the storm?
> While through the tangled corn and yielding clay
> His spurs incessant urge his panting grey*
> 'Tis Vivian, pride of old Cornubias hills
> His veins the untainted blood of Briton fill
> Him follows close a Manners** glorious name;
> In him a Granby's soul aspires to fame
> On such as erst, when Rodney gained the day
> Ebb'd from his kinsman's wound the life away,
> 'Front form the line!' cries Vivian; still its course
> The head maintained; the rear with headlong force
> Speeds at the word, till troops with troops combine
> And each firm squadron forms the serried line.

---

* Hussey Vivian rode a milk-white horse into battle.
** Colonel Lord Robert Manners.

NOTES AND REFERENCES

1. Joseph Roux (ibid.). *Pensées*, p.61, Paris (1886), and quoted by A. C. Grayling in his *Times* column.
2. The 7th Marquess of Anglesey in Hamilton Williams' *Waterloo – New Perspectives* (1993), pp.9 and 10.
3. Philip J. Haythornthwaite, *Wellington's Military Machine* (1996), p.7.
4. Haythornthwaite (op. cit.), p.7.
5. David Hamilton Williams (op. cit.), *Waterloo – New Perspectives* (1993), p.19.
6. The 7th Marquess of Anglesey (ibid.). *One Leg* (1961), pp.103-4.
7. Sir Evelyn Wood (ibid.). 'Cavalry in the Waterloo conflict' (1895). Quoted in Claud Vivian.
8. Claud Vivian (ibid.). *Richard Hussey Vivian – a memoir* (1897), p.320.

Chapter Ten

Influences – Family and Truro

EVEN THOUGH John Vivian and his family were domiciled in Wales for many years, they were careful to retain their Cornishness. For example, Hussey's father was known in south Wales as well as in his home county, by the name which defined his origins, John Vivian of Truro. Then, as we have seen elsewhere in this book, Richard Hussey Vivian, throughout his life, was fiercely loyal to his native county, considered Truro to be his spiritual home, whilst his affiliation with matters Cornish was undimmed by the passage of time. It is true that, after having represented his home town in Westminster for five years, he became MP for Windsor, but that was more to do with health concerns as well as his relationships with members of the Royal Family, than with geographical representation. Even then, he returned to his home county in 1837 when he became MP for East Cornwall, a constituency which he served until his elevation to became Baron Vivian of Glynn and Truro in 1841.

Richard Hussey came from an extremely proud branch of the Vivian family, one influenced by a number of outstanding individuals. For example, his maternal grandmother, Mary Hussey was described by one of her descendants as 'The highest and proudest old lady that ever was'.[1] She was an important figure both in her days as mother and, later as grandmother, for she gave the family that important measure of stability which such leaders exude. She, also, opened doors and, given her background and connections, her networks were invaluable in terms of the quality of education, social skills and professional guidance of her issue. Many influential people were visited with the development of her young people at the forefront of her mind, and she ensured that the representatives of her family behaved in a manner which was conducive to their being received as coming from an equal (or sometimes superior) place in society. That training was invaluable as the children grew up, when the young men and women maintained a presence and followed a code which would stand them in good stead throughout their lives. Mary Hussey had a distinct social advantage over her husband in that her father was a barrister, one of her brothers served as Solicitor General, and a third was a colonel in the army. Colonel Hussey, it was said, inspired young Richard Hussey Vivian (he was barely eighteen at the time) to join the army although, as is clear from the early chapters in this book, that 'reason' was part of a smoke screen utilised by Hussey to gain his father's financial support.

85

Despite that training, Mary's son, John Vivian was not blessed with a warm personality. Indeed, one of his relations said of him that, 'He had never been on sufficiently good terms with anyone to allow anybody to go into his room without knocking.'² Yet, as will be seen, he became betrothed to, and married (at the age of 24) the much and most admired young lady of his day, Betsy Cranch. No doubt, a romantic novelist would make much of the part likely to have been played by Mary Hussey in encouraging the union. Not, that is, that Miss Cranch was unaware of the potential associated with being Mrs. John Vivian of Truro, nor that their relationship was anything but loving. After all, there is nothing new in the observation that the success of opposites in marriage and in business partnerships is not uncommon.

The standard method of naming people, of course, is for the father's surname to be used by the children of a marriage as their family name. In the Vivians' case, the wider family was numerous and, whilst it has not been possible to establish exactly how they decided which individuals were to adopt the second surname, there would appear to be a number of considerations. In the case of the name 'Hussey', for example, there is no doubt that it would be an advantage to the recipient in social circles, it would clearly define the branch of the Vivian clan to which the individual belonged, and, it would help to perpetuate the family name of the mother/grandmother.

John Vivian of Truro, was, without doubt the *paterfamilias* of his branch of the dynasty. He was also a significant figure in the copper industry not only in Cornwall, but also in Wales, and in negotiations on behalf of the Cornish companies, with the mine owners in Anglesey. Furthermore, despite his less than outgoing personality, with his beautiful wife as his consort, he moved in the highest social circles, creating relationships, some of which were to prove beneficial to the career of his eldest son, Richard.

Such was the general perception of the status of the wider Vivian family that, over time, there developed a number of stories relating to the origin of the dynasty. One of these, which some critics argued was nothing more than folklore, was based upon the belief that the genesis of the Vivian family could be traced to an obscure Roman general – *Vivianus Annus*. The general, it was believed, led the invasion of the area before the time of Christ and, in due course, fathered a number of children, who grew up to be the first British-born Vivians. Not surprisingly, the critics of this standpoint provoked a response from the wider family, which sought to defend the veracity of the history as they saw it. Meanwhile, these critics continued to argue that the stories were myths, and there was the danger of them becoming woven into the very fabric of the true history of Cornwall.

It was against this background that John Lambrook Vivian published his *Visitation of the County of Cornwall* (1874), one part of which set out an argument in favour of the *status quo,* which was hardly objective. Lambrook concluded this section of the book with a proclamation which proudly stated (with more than a touch of hyperbole):

'I thus restore the Vivians of Cornwall to their true dignity of descent, a descent from the Roman conquerors of Britain and a dignity not communicable, I believe, to any other family in the whole Island at present'.[3]

This did not satisfy the critics, who conducted further research which, over the years, showed that the name, Vivian, was likely to have been of French or Italian origin and that the earliest record of it, or one of its variants, in Cornwall did not occur until the century following the Norman Conquest. It was the latter which was shown to be the sounder of the two positions. Many years later (1989), Stanley Vivian published *The Story of the Vivians*, a book which had the advantage of fuller research data, which, coupled with less subjective pressure on the author, resulted in a more balanced discussion.[4]

It might be helpful at this stage, to comment briefly on the inclusion of the present discussion in this book. Simply, it is intended to reinforce the reader's understanding of the pride of the Vivian dynasty and of the accompanying ethos which motivated Hussey Vivian to wish to achieve as much as he did in his life-time. In addition, it is to indicate the burning regard which he had for his home county.

Undoubtedly, John Vivian of Truro was the catalyst for what may be thought of as a great leap forward in the standing and the wealth of his family. It is also true that, without that success, it is unlikely that Richard Hussey could have progressed in the army as he did. Born in 1750, it was as a result of the quality of his work in the Cornish metal industry, that in a relatively short time, Vivian of Truro rose rapidly in the hierarchy of the county's business community. He was aided and abetted in this advance by the much admired Betsy Cranch, whom he married when he was 24, and who more than compensated socially for John's rather dour personality. Such was her appeal as a hostess or guest in the county's social circle that a contemporary writer gave it as his opinion that, during her lifetime, 'Truro was full of life and splendour and joy, mainly attributable to her sweet influence'.[5] Whether Betsy's skills included motivating her husband in his progress, or in developing his business vision, can only be based upon conjecture. However, if the old saw is true, that behind a successful man there is always an able woman, then it is highly likely that she did make a contribution.

Among John's major strengths as a manager and businessman was his ability to perceive those changes in the market place which were irreversible, long before other men, and to know which steps should be taken in order to take advantage of the opportunities which were inherent in the changed market. In copper smelting, given the economic advantages which south Wales enjoyed over many other parts of the country, coupled with the severe disadvantages and uncertainties which Cornwall was having to face, John Vivian reasoned that he should move his business interests to the coastal strip of south-west Wales. He was not short of 'suitors' who wished to take advantage of his knowledge, expertise and business skills. Among the companies for whom he had acted as agent in Cornwall, was the Birmingham firm, The Cheadle Company. After some frank discussion, Vivian agreed to join Cheadle as a partner in their relatively small copper smelting operation based at the coastal town of Penclawdd, which is to the west of Swansea on the Gower Coast. It was his skills in purchasing copper ore which gave the partnership an initial edge over its rivals, but John could not see such advantage in the longer term which could sustain the firm's competitive position in the market. In the meantime he made the astute appointment of his twenty-one-year-old son, John Henry, as works manager at the Penclawdd plant. It was a decision which provided the young man with a personal development opportunity under his father's tutelage, and helped prepare him for the role which he would play as a result of the Vivians' decision to open the Hafod plant.

During this period whilst Hussey was a serving soldier, he did not get involved with the day-to-day running of the family business. Indeed, in his many letters to family and friends he rarely referred to the family enterprise, and was an infrequent visitor to Swansea. As has been discussed, his father continued to hope that, one day, Richard Hussey Vivian would take his place around the Vivian board table. As late as 1810, when the Hafod works was established, John Vivian of Truro allocated shares in the business in equal proportion to Hussey and his brother John Henry Vivian (25 per cent each), while retaining 50 per cent himself. Nevertheless, on occasion, Hussey did represent his father at various business meetings in Cornwall, and he showed himself to be a competent committee member. In addition he gave advice to his brother regarding important decisions which had to be made which affected the Hafod business. It is reported that he:

> '. . . displayed a wide knowledge of business . . . but he was not the originator of business ideas . . .'[6]

Interestingly, though, when the Mona Mine Company was acquired, the list of partners included J. H. Vivian, Lord Uxbridge and Lt.-Colonel Hussey Vivian.

When Hussey returned to Truro at the end of his military service, he was fêted. In the eyes of the citizens of the Cornish town, he was a 'local boy' who had been transformed into a dashing hero who had fought with Wellington at Waterloo. Furthermore, he had moved in the highest social circles, and was a close friend of the Prince of Wales. Yet, when he stood as candidate in the Westminster election, he was defeated by 12 votes to 11. Disappointed as he was, his spirits were lifted when his supporters carried him shoulder high to his father's house. That collective spirit was nurtured over time, and Hussey and his supporters were much better prepared when the next election came around and, on that occasion he was the successful candidate, and entered Parliament to represent Truro.

In presenting a biography of an individual, it would be less than honest to ignore, or seek to hide any perceived blemishes in the person's character. For example, his critics would point to what they might describe as, his 'relentless' pursuit of promotion, honours and elevation to the most influential circles in society. Others would mention his apparent weakness for gambling which, in the eyes of some, was encouraged by his close relationship with members of the Royal Family. Hussey's fondness for the company of attractive young ladies might be another topic of speculation and comment. One author, when following this line of argument, left no room for conjecture when he informed his readers that Hussey Vivian had fathered 'at least one' illegitimate child.[7]

Without wishing to condone or decry any of these activities, in considering historical situations, it is important to view behaviour in the context of the times in which the 'actors' live. In Hussey's case, it is interesting to quote the original Vivian family motto. It was *Dum vivimus vivamus* (while we live, let us live). It could be said that, if the foregoing charges are valid, that Hussey did his best to live up to the spirit and the meaning of those words. Against that, his focus on duty was more powerful than any of his weaknesses, though that is not to say that he was not fond of the ladies, which, for an attractive man in his position in society might have led to dalliances which, it would appear, were the norm at that time. In effect, the mores of society then were as different as those who grew up before the Sixties find to be evident today. For the army officer of the time there was also another issue which should be noted. In ongoing conditions of war there was always the possibility of being killed. This fact must have affected the frame of mind which reflected the Vivian motto quoted above, for it would appear that few army officers led celibate lives. Furthermore, judging by some of Hussey's letters to his wife,[8] written during the campaigns in the Peninsula and in France, she was probably aware of the temptations presented to him and accepted his succumbing to them as inevitable. Whilst neither of the examples given offers explicit proof, it is difficult to understand why Hussey should introduce the subject in the way he did, unless there was some truth behind the innuendo.

There is also a related issue which should be mentioned here, regarding the letters which Hussey and his military comrades wrote to family and friends during the Peninsular and French campaigns. Judging by Hussey's letters, no form of censorship was then in operation. It is interesting to speculate whether such topics would have been included in outgoing letters from the battlefields had some form of control been in place. In addition, why was it that the military organisations allowed soldiers to give detailed descriptions of their activities, the routes taken, the strength of their force and other information which would be beneficial to the enemy? In the context of the wars waged in the twentieth century that would have been inconceivable, and there is no reason to believe that Napoleon failed to take advantage of the availability of such a rich seam of intelligence.

Hussey had married his first wife, Eliza, when he was twenty-nine. It is said that the couple had eloped to Gretna Green (though that has not been confirmed), and that neither set of parents approved of the union, but there was little that they could do about it, and, in due course, following the birth of his two sons, John and Charles, there was rapprochement. Then came a double blow which staggered Hussey. First his father John Vivian of Truro was killed in a hunting accident, and then his wife passed away.

Several years earlier, in 1825, Hussey had been appointed to the post of Inspector-General of Cavalry and served in that role until 1830. During his tenure (in 1827) he was promoted to the rank of Lieutenant-General and became Colonel of the Prince of Wales' Royal Lancers, and in 1831 he was made Commander of British forces in Ireland. Unfortunately, his wife's health began to deteriorate, causing him to retire from Parliament before he went to Ireland. In the same year his wife died. However, Hussey was not destined to be a widower for long. After seeking solace in the company of the daughter of an Anglican clergyman, Leticia Webster, her father married the couple who, in the short time they had together, were blessed with a baby girl (Lalage).

Although Hussey had some concern about his own health, it was in 1835 that he was appointed to a post which he had long sought; he became Master-General of Ordnance and, soon after, was made a Privy Counsellor and Knight Grand Cross of the Bath. Sadly, his health continued to deteriorate and, soon after taking his seat in the House of Lords, he was advised by his doctors to take the waters in Baden-Baden, the German spa town. The treatment, however, was ineffective and he passed away far from his beloved Truro. His last journal entry provides us with a portrait of a man preparing himself to meet his maker. He wrote:

> 'After a short walk, the pain in my chest and arms was beyond any I
> have before felt . . . God's will be done. I hope when the time comes
> I shall meet my end as becomes a man and a soldier, and that God,
> in their distress, will support my dear wife, my children, and my
> family'.[9]

The news of Hussey Vivian's death (on 20 August 1842) was received with great sorrow, not only throughout Cornwall but also in the many avenues along which he had travelled during his lifetime. Not surprisingly, the eulogy published in the *West Briton* newspaper gave expression to the feelings of loss which the news had brought to his birthplace. The Grim Reaper had gathered-in an outstanding Cornishman who had come through many valleys where death was much more than a shadow. But the memory of this son of Truro was to remain in the minds of his fellow townsfolk long after his death.

The *West Briton* tribute focused upon a rich life of service and duty. The following excerpt exemplifies the warmth of feeling which flows through the whole piece:

> 'The attachment of a grateful heart to early associations was universally appreciated . . . how distinguished his career, how kind his feelings, how well he conferred a favour, or, if beyond his power to grant, with what tact and kindness he softened the denial'.[10]

The paper continued in this vein before commenting upon his allegiance to his home county and to the reciprocal feelings of his fellow townsmen, for many of whom Hussey was an idol. The writer of the eulogy stressed Hussey's 'love for Cornwall' describing it as 'something we must not forget'. He also urged the county to commemorate in some appropriate fashion, the life of 'the most distinguished man Cornwall had given birth to in recent times'.

In accordance with his desires, Hussey's body was taken to St. Mary's Church (now incorporated in Truro Cathedral), where it was interred near his mother and father in the Vivian family vault. Hussey had also requested that the funeral should be conducted, as far as possible, in a private and unpretentious manner. He wanted the whole process to be as near as possible to that which had been adopted for the funeral of his father. The Mayor, however, felt that, taking cognisance of Hussey Vivian's request, that Truro's citizens should have the opportunity to express their affectionate remembrance of, and pride in the man whom some called 'The Warrior of the West'. As a consequence, it was agreed that all shops and businesses should be closed from 10 o'clock until 1 o'clock on the day of the funeral.

The thoughts of those who lined the route taken by the funeral procession, or who sat in the pews at St. Mary's waiting for the formal service to begin, might well have contrasted the sorrow of the day with that of Richard Hussey Vivian's homecoming following the glorious victory at Waterloo, Then, Truro had been *en fête*, when, in their enthusiasm to welcome their home town hero, a group of young men had released the horses from Hussey's carriage, took their place themselves and pulled the vehicle to its destination, his father's house. It was a glorious day. As he surveyed the cheering throng, Hussey must have felt the strength of the bond between himself and his fellow townsfolk. It was that bond which provided a modicum of solace for the mourners on the day of his burial.

In researching and writing this book, the author has been conscious of the fact that any biography represents its author's interpretation of his subject and those with whom he came in contact. As the reader will have noted from earlier discussion, some who have written about Richard Hussey Vivian have been critical of him in one respect or another. This is not surprising, for very few men have led blameless lives and Hussey was not one of them. On the other hand, few have achieved so many praiseworthy goals and have been rewarded with such recognition of his achievements as he. After delving deeply into the sources of this remarkable man's history, the author of this biography's is firmly of the opinion that, in the case of Richard Hussey Vivian, the positives far outweigh the negatives.

Perhaps the final sentences of W. H. Tregelles's paper on Hussey Vivian best sum up the character and standing of the Cornish hero. Tregelles quotes a Dr. Wolcot, whom he describes as 'No lenient critic', who said of Hussey that he was:

> 'An excellent officer, and better still, a kind, brave, honourable and good man'.

Certainly he was a man who, as the *West Briton* eulogy urged, should not be forgotten.

He was a true Cornish hero!

NOTES AND REFERENCES

1. Sally Jones (ibid.), 'The Vivian family', in *Transactions of the Port Talbot Historical Society*, Vol. 2, No. 3 (1974), p.5.
2. Sally Jones (op. cit.), p.6.
3. John Lambrook Vivian (ibid.), *Visitation of the County of Cornwall* (1874).
4. Stanley Vivian (ibid.). *The Story of the Vivians* (1989).
5. Stanley Vivian (op. cit.), p.40.
6. Ralph A. Griffiths (ibid.), *Singleton Abbey and the Vivians in Swansea* (1988), p.15.
7. Ralph A. Griffiths (op. cit.), p.14.
8. In Claud Vivian (ibid.), *Richard Hussey Vivian – A Memoir*, p.73 – a letter dated November 1808:

   > 'Lieut.-General Lord P was quartered upon the house of a colonel serving with the Gallician army. His wife – a pretty woman was remarkably civil to us. At the Colonel's house was a friend of his wife, an exceedingly loquacious sort of lady, in whose company I should very soon have attained the Spanish language'.

   And another dated October 1813, p.147:

   > 'I shall lament leaving this, for the quarters I now occupy are most excellent . . . but no pretty girls, which I lament as it assists me in learning Spanish . . . I should tell you that to make up for the want of pretty girls in my house, the cousins of my patroness . . . two most beautiful creatures, pay me a visit each breakfast-time, and sit and chat for an hour or two . . .'

9. Claud Vivian (op. cit.). Extract from Hussey's last entry in his journal.
10. The *West Briton* reporting the funeral on 13 September 1842.
11. W. H. Tregelles in *Cornish Worthies*, Volume 2 (1884), pp.343-364.

Bibliography

Sir Archibald Alison, *History of Europe*, Edinburgh (1860).

Marquess of Anglesey, *One Leg*, London (1961).

Marquess of Anglesey, *A History of British Cavalry*, Volume One (1971).

Lorraine A. Cook, 'The Vivians of Cornwall', in *Minerva* IV (1996).

Ralph A., Griffiths, *Singleton Abbey and the Vivians of Swansea* (1988).

Lt.-Colonel Gurwood, *The Despatches of Wellington XI1266* (1837).

P. J. Haythornthwaite, *Wellington's Military Machine*, Tunbridge Wells (1989).

P. J. Haythornthwaite, *The Armies of Wellington*, London (1996).

D. C. Hamilton-Williams, *Waterloo – New Perspectives*, London (1993).

Richard Holmes, *Wellington*, London (2003).

Stephen Hughes, *Copperopolis*, Aberystwyth (2000).

Sally Jones, *The Vivian Family*, Port Talbot History Society (1974).

T. H. McGuffie, *The Siege of Gibraltar*, London (1965).

Sir Charles Petrie, *Wellington – A Reassessment*, London (1956).

Joseph Roux, *Pensées*, Paris (1886).

W. H. Tregelles, *Some Cornish Worthies*, Volume II (1894).

R. R. Twoomey, 'A study of the firm in the copper and related industries', University of Wales, Swansea. Ph.D. thesis, Swansea (1979).

Claud Vivian, *Richard Hussey Vivian – A Memoir* (1897).

Stanley Vivian, *The Story of the Vivians* (1989).

J. Lambrook Vivian, *Visitation of the County of Cornwall* (1874).

Jac Weller, *Wellington at Waterloo*, London (1967).

J. Steven Watson, *The Reign of George III*, Oxford (1959).

Index

During the period covered by this book, two of the leading figures in the story acquired new titles. Sir Arthur Wellesley became the Duke of Wellington and was given the sobriquet 'The Iron Duke'. Whilst he did not acquire a nickname until Waterloo, Lord Paget first, became Lord Uxbridge and, then, the First Marquess of Anglesey. (Note that the author credited with several references with extracts under this title is the seventh Marquess.)